Arden's Housing Library

Andrew Arden QC and **Caroline Hunter** are the Series Editors of Arden's Housing Library. The team of expert authors is drawn from the members of Arden Chambers and other practitioners.

Arden's Housing Library provides accessible guidance to the details of housing rights and duties for those involved in the management of social housing. It breaks up the whole subject into digestible segments and approaches each topic from the perspective of its practical application. Information about other titles in the Library is given at the back of this book.

Caroline Hunter is a barrister and senior lecturer in law at Sheffield Hallam University. She is the joint Series Editor of Arden's Housing Library and author of *Tenants' Rights* and (with Andy Selman) *CCT of Housing Management* in that series.

Kerry Bretherton is a practising barrister at Arden Chambers in London, specialising is housing, landlord and tenant, and local government law.

Anti-social Behaviour

Law and Practice
in the Management
of Social Housing

Caroline Hunter, Barrister
and **Kerry Bretherton,** Barrister

Lemos&**Crane**

First published in Great Britain 1998 by
Lemos & Crane
20 Pond Square
Highgate
London N6 6BA

© Caroline Hunter and Kerry Bretherton, 1998

ISBN 1-898001-37-5

A CIP catalogue record for this book is available from
the British Library

Text design by Mick Keates, London
Formatting by Concise Artisans, London
Cover design by DAP Ltd, London
Printed and bound by Redwood Books, Trowbridge

Contents

Series Foreword

By **Andrew Arden, QC**

What is housing law?

Housing law, put simply, is about the respective rights and duties of the owners and occupiers of housing. (Although Arden's Housing Library is concerned only with rented housing – whether leasehold or tenanted – the term 'housing law' applies across the board: thus, as a mortgage is a legal interest in land, a mortgagee [building society or bank] qualifies as an owner [of that interest], just as much as the outright owner of his or her own home will also be its occupier). As with all forms of law, the evolution of housing law is governed not merely by what Parliament lays down, but also by the way the law comes to be applied, understood and accepted, through individual cases. To understand a subject, then, requires knowledge both of the content of the law, and of how it works in practice.

Development of housing law

The development of housing law as a subject was largely based on rights of occupation and so tended to be addressed to the occupiers of housing and their advisers. This was not an approach that exclusively benefited occupiers: as with all forms of enforcement, each individual action (or reaction) on the part of an occupier contained an element that was – at its lowest – informative to the owner, or else that served to develop the law in its application, comprehension and acceptance, for occupiers and owners alike. It was not unknown, nor was it improper, for landlords – in particular, local authorities – to fund agencies to assist tenants to take action against themselves, in part in their own interests, ie, so that they would learn from it, and/or that the strengths and weaknesses of institutional practices could be tested.

Need for a new approach

With the reduction in rights of occupation (in both the private sector, and housing associations), and – increasingly – reduced access to legal advice (with greater reductions yet to come as a result of the proposed changes to legal aid), however, the use of an adversarial, case-by-case approach to the development and understanding of housing law has become a much less reliable approach: unsatisfactory conditions, or systems, or mere errors of law, may be allowed to prosper and proliferate because there is no one with a sufficient interest, or else with the necessary access to assistance, to point out a relevant mistake or its consequences – in other words, quite literally, mistakes may go unchecked.

It has accordingly become more important for housing managers to ensure that their actions are legally correct from the outset, instead of relying on a corrective response from occupiers; put another way, the move away from litigation at the suit of the tenant creates a correspondingly greater need for managerial prevention of error within the landlord institution. At the same time, the courts have come to expect a high level of knowledge of, and respect for, individual rights, including in the area of housing: when managers get it wrong, and the occupier has the recourse to legal assistance to get the matter into court, errors tend to be extremely expensive – in damages or compensation, and in legal costs – which in turn adds to the financial burden on the providers of social housing and exacerbates the difficulty of getting it right in the first place.

Put thus, the need for greater awareness of housing

rights, on the part of housing managers, sounds exclusively self-interested. Those who go into professions within social housing, however, usually do so because, in one way or another, they wish to see an improvement in living conditions for those least able to provide for themselves. It is not merely in their interests – financial or institutional – to 'get it right' for occupiers, but a central part of their purpose. For much the same reasons – reduced rights, reduced access to assistance in enforcing them – it is, therefore, also important to housing managers to enjoy a heightened awareness of the rights of occupiers, from this additional, and alternative, perspective.

Books for housing managers

The Housing Library that bears my name is aimed at those whose daily work involves knowledge of the respective legal rights and duties of landlords and tenants in the social housing sector (meaning stock owned or controlled by bodies such as local authorities, housing associations and trusts, Housing Action Trusts, management agencies, and tenant management organisations). It is aimed at those who have gone into social housing because they are concerned to ensure that tenants enjoy the best of housing rights, yet who, paradoxically, may find themselves – in a considerably less liberal climate than prevailed in the formative years of post-war social housing – needing to enforce landlords' rights against tenants as much as, if not more than, the other way around. The Housing Library, accordingly, seeks to strike a balance between the rights and duties of landlords and the rights and duties of tenants: the touchstone is good housing management under law.

In some ways, it is easier to define those at whom the series is not directed than those at whom it is, not least because job titles, departmental organisations and structures, and the allocation of specific tasks, all vary from one landlord to another.

One thing that may swiftly be said is that this is not a series of books for lawyers, law students or legal advisers (landlords' or tenants'), but – emphatically – for housing practitioners. The substantial legal texts which are available (including Arden & Partington's Housing Law, the looseleaf second edition of which is additionally co-authored by Caroline Hunter, my co-editor in this series) – and even the shorter legal texts which are concerned with only a single aspect of housing law, for example, homelessness, harassment, security, disrepair, or with an overview of the subject as a whole (Manual of Housing Law) – are, however, not only difficult to get hold of, and relatively costly, but require both a degree of legal expertise or training, and (perhaps above all) considerable time, to apply them to each problem that arises; they are, it may be said, on one or other of these grounds inaccessible to housing managers.

Nor is this a series of books for those who formulate housing policy: while policy-makers (whether central or local) of course need to be familiar with housing rights and duties, they rarely need the detail of how such rights and duties are applied and enforced. Similarly, those whose concern is with housing finance will not commonly need to be on top of the way each last pound is to be spent, inherent in which will certainly be questions of individual issues of disrepair, compensation, disturbance costs and so on. This is not to say that any of these limbs of housing as a subject are entirely separate from each other, merely that in the discharge of different responsibilities, people need to have – and may only want to have – a limited amount (or 'block') of knowledge to hand: more may clutter the issue, or use up a limited amount of time digging out what is relevant and how it fits into a larger picture.

Housing managers, however, and in direct contrast, do need to have a general familiarity both with the detail of housing rights and duties, and with how they fit into a larger whole. What is more, inevitably under pressure, they need to be able to access it swiftly and straightforwardly. Consider this – simplistic but none the less common – example: eviction threatened (or actioned) for some minor cause, provoking either a counterclaim for disrepair which will cost the landlord considerably more than was to be gained in the first place, or perhaps an attempt to exercise the right to buy a property (which, in turn, interferes with a major development proposal, impacting on a financial allocation which is dependent on ability to deliver within a tight time-table). Or, again, a refusal to repair something within the landlord's obligations, on account of a planned maintenance programme (which has the effect of elevating local proposals above the law and, of course, is ineffective).

What the Housing Library does, therefore, is to break up the subject (so far as relevant) into digestible segments, and to approach each segment from the perspective of its practical application. Familiarity with the series as a whole, and extensive cross-reference between its titles, will result in a whole package.

Conclusion

All those who work in social housing want to provide the best housing conditions that are affordable, to those least able to provide it for themselves; this is not merely a question of physical conditions, but of the ability to enjoy peace and security in the home, freedom from interference and oppression, and the right to make the very most of it that is compatible with the general interest. While the managers of social housing may volunteer additional rights, they are bound to comply with the minimum requirements of the law, and any management policy or philosophy that does not do so will be doomed to fail.

Alexander Pope said that a little knowledge is a dangerous thing. I say, it is still better than none; and, the best way to build it up into a substantial body of knowledge is in manageable stages! I hope that, in housing, this series will make a contribution.

Table of Cases

Table of Statutes

Table of Statutory Instruments

Introduction

It is impossible to be certain whether the extent of anti-social behaviour by tenants has increased over the last 15 years. Nonetheless the perception of those involved in social housing is that it has become more of a problem. Without effective monitoring no-one knows exactly how much more of a problem, or indeed whether increased awareness has simply led to increased reporting of a problem that already existed. But what can be said with certainty is that 15 years ago it was not a question that rated very highly in terms of housing management priorities. All that has now changed.

How to deal with anti-social behaviour is not just an issue for housing managers. It is now also a matter taken up by national politicians and media. The White Paper on Housing ('Our Future Homes', Cm. 2901) issued in June 1995 acknowledged (p. 43) that 'the anti-social behaviour of neighbours and others can, ...cause misery for the responsible majority of tenants.' The change in opinion has been so great that the 1996 Housing Act directly addressed the problem. One striking feature of the coverage, and indeed the new legislation, is that it is generally tenants of social landlords and particularly local authority landlords, who are targeted as the perpetrators of this anti-social behaviour. Again it is very difficult to be certain how far this portrayal is true, and, if it is, whether this is due to the increasing residualisation of the sector or other social forces. The approach of the Crime and Disorder Act 1998 has been to target all perpetrators of anti-social behaviour.

While it is difficult to be sure about the reasons for this apparent increase in anti-social behaviour (one might even argue that it can be linked to the granting of security of tenure in 1980), some causes of particular problems can be isolated. One such factor is the increasing number of vulnerable people being housed by social landlords through the care in the community programme. Such people may be both the perpetrators and the victims of anti-social behaviour, yet the increased management time necessitated by such tenants is often overlooked.

For many years social landlords believed that 'neighbour disputes' were not a matter for them. After all, some might argue that it is paternalistic to suggest that tenants – unlike, say, owner-occupiers – are unable to deal with such disputes for themselves. On the other hand, to take such an attitude was to leave many tenants without any effective mechanism for dealing with anti-social behaviour, and failed to recognise the serious problems being caused, and the real risk that what might start as a minor issue could develop into a major incident. Over the last ten years the attitude of many social landlords has changed: with an increasing incidence of complaints, anti-social behaviour is no longer an issue that can be ignored. By 1993 it was estimated by that 20 per cent of front-line housing officers' time was spent dealing with 'problem' tenants (*Managing Neighbour Complaints in Social Housing: A Handbook for Practitioners*, Aldbourne Associates).

What is meant by anti-social behaviour?

Definitions of anti-social behaviour vary widely. The most commonly quoted definition, which embraces a wide range of behaviour, is given by Legg *et al* (*Could Local Authorities Be Better Landlords*, Housing Research Group, City University, London, 1981). It states at p. 14:

> "There are annoying but relatively minor events like children playing games in unauthorised areas; there are also the serious matters such as burglaries, muggings and racial harassment. In between these two extremes there is a wide variety... noise is a constant source of complaints in many areas."

Government pronouncements, on the other hand, have tended to concentrate solely on the criminal end of anti-social behaviour. This is exemplified in the new injunction powers in the Housing Act 1996, which deal only with cases or actual or threatened violence.

In this book we have tried to encompass a wide-range of behaviour. It is very difficult to come up with an objective definition that draws a line between 'behaviour that opposes society's norms and accepted standards of behaviour' (the definition used by the Chartered Institute of Housing in its *Housing Management Standards Manual*). So while our broad approach will always run the risk of categorising as 'anti-social' behaviour which is in no way deviant, and which in other circumstances (for example, of different building design and layout) might be perfectly acceptable, it does recognise that what is anti-social is to a certain extent subjective and has to be viewed from the victim's point of view.

Surveys of tenants have suggested that, perhaps unsurprisingly, the majority of complaints do not focus on serious criminal activity, but on more recurrent activities such as noise and litter. A survey by Camden London Borough Council of 1,300 tenants carried out between October 1995 and January 1996 found that a third had experienced some form of neighbour nuisance in the previous 12 months, and that noise was the most common form of nuisance. This is similar to an earlier study by Salford University of local authority and housing association tenants where noise was again the most common form of complaint (see V. Karn, R. Lickiss, D. Hughes and J. Crawley, *Neighbour Disputes: Responses by Social Landlords*, Institute of Housing, 1993). Other major sources of complaint in both studies were pets (principally dogs) and rubbish or litter.

Outline of the book

The primary concern of this book is the legal remedies open to social landlords in dealing with anti-social behaviour. Legal remedies cannot, however, be seen in isolation from other policies to deal with such behaviour. It is important that they are seen as part of a comprehensive policy. Accordingly in Chapter 1 we set out briefly our views on the contents and nature of such a policy, and in particular seek to emphasise the importance of a multi-agency approach, an approach that now has statutory backing in the Crime and Disorder Act 1998.

There are many reasons why landlords should seek to address the issue of anti-social behaviour, but perhaps most compelling (from the landlord's point of view) are the efforts now being made by some of the victims of anti-social behaviour to sue their landlords for the damages they have suffered. There appears to be an increasing number of cases brought against landlords for this type of damage, and in Chapter 2 we examine the existing law and consider how it may develop.

One of the specific measures included in the 1996 Act to deal with anti-social behaviour is the 'introductory tenancy' for local authority landlords. Whether authorities wish to adopt such measures as part of their overall policy is considered in Chapter 1. The detailed operation of introductory tenancies is considered in Chapter 3.

Anti-social behaviour may be categorised both by the nature of the perpetrator of the behaviour and by the type of behaviour. At the risk of some overlap, we have sought to approach the issue from both points of view. Chapters 4 and 5 consider the issue from the point of view of *who* the perpetrator is. Chapter 4 deals with anti-social behaviour by the tenant him or herself, while Chapter 5 concerns non-tenant perpetrators whether adults or children and also the particular problems of owner-occupier and vulnerable perpetrators.

Chapters 6 and 7 concern the nature of the behaviour. Chapter 6 looks at a range of activity from violence and drug-dealing to pets. Chapter 7 separates out the particular issues which arise when anti-social behaviour is motivated by race or other prejudices.

Finally, Chapter 8 is concerned with the practical problems of bringing cases to court and the steps that need to be taken to ensure successful outcomes.

Crime and Disorder Act 1998

While working on this book the Labour Government introduced the Crime and Disorder Bill with specific, essentially criminal sanctions, targeted at anti-social behaviour. The Bill became an Act while the book was in its final stages. We have incorporated the provisions at various relevant stages through the book, although at the time of writing none had yet been brought into force and detailed guidance on their workings was awaited.

I.
Providing a Comprehensive Approach

Allocation, re-housing and homelessness /
Physical environment / Employment policies /
Youth services / Crime and disorder strategies /
Housing management policies and procedures /
Inter-agency working

Although this book is primarily concerned with the *legal* remedies that are available to social landlords to deal with anti-social behaviour, these cannot be seen in isolation and must be used as part of a comprehensive approach to the problem. So consideration should be given not only to day-to-day management questions, but also of broader issues of strategy. In order to develop an effective strategy, consideration must be given to the whole range of housing functions of the landlord, and even beyond this to incorporate employment and youth policies. The first part of this chapter looks at issues of wider strategy and the second part, housing management best practice.

Allocation, re-housing and homelessness

Allocation to permanent local authority housing and nominations by authorities to registered social landlords is now controlled by Part VI of the Housing Act (HA)1996. One issue which local authorities must consider is whether they will exclude those guilty of anti-social behaviour from their stock. This may be achieved in one of two ways:

1. by simply making those who have been evicted for, or are otherwise guilty of, anti-social behaviour ineligible as persons who are not 'qualified' under section 161(4) of HA 1996;
2. by giving a lower priority under section 167 to such persons, so that even if they otherwise come within the priority categories of section 167 they obtain a low priority.

In both cases it is necessary to have mechanisms which allow for consideration of the particular applicant's circumstances, but in general there is no reason why such policies should not be adopted.

For registered social landlords, there is less control of their own direct waiting list policies, and they may certainly seek to exclude those who have a record of anti-social behaviour. There seems to be growing evidence of landlords sharing information on tenants who are guilty of anti-social behaviour in order to exclude them from social housing. In parts of inner city Salford it has been reported that housing associations and private landlords have swapped information (*Inside Housing*, 1 May 1998).

Landlords may also wish to exclude tenants from any priority for transfer when legal action is being contemplated for anti-social behaviour.

Case report

Mr and Mrs Wilson were secure tenants of a property owned by York City Council, which they occupied with their three sons. A number of allegations concerning nuisance were made about the whole family, and the authority served a notice of intention to seek possession. In accordance with the authority's

procedures an internal appeal was heard against the decision. The report to the internal appeal committee set out three possible options: repossession, management transfer, or allowing the Wilsons to stay in their own home. The committee decided to proceed with the eviction and the letter informing the Wilsons of this also stated that the authority would not consider re-housing as a solution. The Wilsons sought judicial review of the decision to refuse to transfer them. The court decided that the individual merits of the case had been considered, and the decision reached was a reasonable one. *R v York City Council, ex p Wilson* (1996)

Beyond the exclusion of certain people altogether, consideration also needs to be given to using allocation policies to try to foster a greater sense of community on particular problem estates. Given the inherent flexibility in Part VI of HA 1996 there is no reason why local authorities, as well as registered social landlords should not attempt this for particular areas. Thus on the Vikinglea area of the Manor Estate in Sheffield the usual needs-based allocation system was abandoned by North British Housing Association in favour of advertising in the local press for people who 'wanted to build a new community'. The adverts 'were aimed at people who had housing need, but were not necessarily in the greatest need'. Applicants had to agree to police checks being run and about half were rejected. (See further *Inside Housing*, 13 June 1997: pp. 16-17.)

While eviction procedures may be successful in obtaining possession against those responsible for anti-social behaviour, the question always remains whether they should then be re-housed once homeless. For registered social landlords this may be less of a problem than for local authorities that also have duties towards the homeless under what is now Part VII of HA 1996. Where the tenant is not in priority need (i.e. because he or she has no children or is not vulnerable) then there is no difficulty in rejecting any application for substantive assistance under Part VII. Where the tenant has children or is vulnerable then a view has to be taken on intentional homelessness. It is important that staff working in the homelessness section are not operating in isolation from the remainder of the housing department, so that while each individual case is considered on its merits, authorities should ensure that there is a co-ordinated and consistent response to such applicants. It is open to authorities to find that applicants who have been evicted for anti-social conduct are intentionally homeless, even where the trouble has been caused by their children (see e.g. *R v Salford City Council ex p Devenport* (1983)). In a high profile case, where neighbours had made hundreds of complaints, one family was evicted by Manchester City Council. The authority then found the family to be intentionally homeless (*Inside Housing*, 19 April 1996). Moreover, as the next case report shows someone may even be vulnerable and yet intentionally homeless.

Case report

Ms Bell was a secure tenant of Wirral Metropolitan Borough Council. Between 1991 and 1993 a number of injunctions were taken out to restrain her anti-social conduct. In November 1993 a suspended possession order was obtained against her, subject to various conditions relating to her future conduct. She failed to comply with the conditions and possession was obtained. Ms Bell accordingly applied to the council as homeless. The council concluded that she was homeless and in priority need, due to her mental health problems. It also concluded, however, that she was intentionally homeless.

Although the council had found that her mental health problems caused her to be vulnerable, the court found no inconsistency between this and the finding of intentionality. That finding had been based on the Homelessness Code of Guidance, which stated that an applicant's conduct should not

> be regarded as deliberate (and therefore inten-
> tional) if he or she is 'incapable of managing his/her
> affairs, for example on account of old age, or mental
> illness or handicap'. This, the court concluded, was a
> different test from that of vulnerability, and one on
> which there was adequate evidence for the con-
> clusion reached by the authority that Ms Bell could
> manage her own affairs.
> *R v Wirral Metropolitan Borough Council ex p Bell*
> (1994)

Physical environment

Another factor that must be considered is the physical environment. It has long been recognised that housing and
estate design can play a part in mediating behaviour. Where
new build, conversion or major rehabilitation works are
being carried out, thought should be given to issues of tenant
nuisance. In particular sound insulation should be a priority.
In high rise blocks consideration may be given to the intro-
duction of concierge schemes (see further, J. Farr and
S. Osborn, *High Hopes: concierge, controlled entry and similar
schemes for high rise blocks*, Safe Neighbourhoods Unit).

For existing properties there is a number of physical
measures which may be taken. These include security
measures such as alarms and also the installation of closed
circuit television in appropriate locations. These 'target hard-
ening' measures may help to deter anti-social behaviour.

Employment policies

Many estates and areas which suffer from severe problems
of anti-social behaviour also suffer from severe economic
deprivation, with high unemployment rates particularly
amongst the young. Strategies to deal with economic depri-

vation may well also help to eradicate problems of anti-social behaviour. The 'Housing Plus' strategies of some housing associations show what can be done amongst registered social landlords.

Youth services

Some young people indulge in anti-social behaviour simply because they have time on their hands. One element of provision that may be worth reviewing, when seeking to take a comprehensive approach to anti-social behaviour is that of youth services. What facilities are there for young people to use? Are they affordable for the young people being targeted? As a non-statutory service, youth services have been cut considerably over the last ten years, and authorities may wish to ask whether this is a false economy.

Crime and disorder strategies

The Crime and Disorder Act 1998, sections 5 and 6, place a three-yearly duty on local authorities, together with the chief police officer for their area to review patterns of crime and disorder and to formulate and implement a strategy for their reduction. In exercising these functions the local authority and chief police officer must co-operate with the police authority, the probation committee, the health authority, and other participants listed by the Secretary of State operating in their area. It is likely that at least some registered social landlords will be amongst those named by the Secretary of State.

The reduction of anti-social behaviour on housing estates will clearly need to be part of this strategy. Most authorities have already commenced their review in preparation for what seems likely to be an initial April 1999 deadline.

The primary focus of this book is on the day-to-day management of social housing and the role of legal remedies within this. A number of issues must be addressed in order that a successful policy can be implemented. It is to the question of housing management best practice that we must now turn.

Housing management policies and procedures

The Housing Management Standards Manual produced by the Chartered Institute of Housing advises that housing organisations should have policies and procedures (drawn up in consultation with tenants) for dealing with nuisance problems caused by tenants and their visitors. While this may seem self-evident, it is surprising how many social landlords do not have a written policy. In Scotland, for example, in 1996 only 55 per cent of local authority landlords had a written policy to deal with neighbour nuisance (there has been no equivalent survey in England and Wales). It is almost impossible for staff to react consistently and appropriately unless there is written documentation outlining the various steps to be taken and advising on their appropriateness in different circumstances.

Having a proper procedure which is followed also protects councils from accusations of improper conduct by alleged perpetrators. Where clear guidelines are set down staff will know for example, when and in what circumstances alleged perpetrators should be interviewed. Once a proper policy is in place it is important that it is followed. Failure to do so may lead to complaints by both victims and alleged perpetrators.

> **Case report**
>
> The London Borough of Tower Hamlets summonsed two female tenants to court on charges of racial harassment without either warning them or interviewing them. The allegations were found to be

unsubstantiated. Both women complained to the ombudsman, who found that the council had not complied with its own procedures. The ombudsman called on the council to pay each woman £500 to remedy a 'serious injustice' plus £250 each for their time and trouble in pursuing the complaint. (*Inside Housing*, 24 April 1998: p. 6)

Tenancy conditions

One aspect of many of the reviews of policy and procedures undertaken by social landlords is that they have looked again at their tenancy conditions. One of the reasons why there may be difficulties in achieving effective legal action against anti-social tenants is that the tenancy agreement may not be sufficiently clearly and strongly worded. At both Coventry City Council and Camden London Borough Council, when they undertook a review of their policy, the first matter considered was the terms of their tenancy agreements. In both cases the terms were altered in the light of the review. Where tenancy terms are altered this may take some time. It is essential to ensure that the legal requirements of the Housing Act 1985 are complied with where tenancies are secure, and that where tenancies are assured the tenants' agreement is obtained (see further C. Hunter, *Tenants' Rights* (Arden's Housing Library) 1995: Ch. 4). The particular terms that might be adopted are considered throughout the book in relation to particular perpetrators and types of behaviour.

Introductory tenancies

Another matter that now has to be reviewed by local authorities when considering policy is whether to adopt an introductory tenancy scheme (the operation of which is set out in Chapter 3 below). However, an initial decision has to be made about whether to adopt one at all. A survey by the

Social Landlords' Crime and Nuisance Group has shown that take-up has not been widespread in the first few months of the scheme. Only 12.4 per cent of authorities had adopted introductory tenancy schemes, while 45.6 per cent had decided not to. The remaining authorities were either intending to adopt a scheme in the future (15 per cent) or were still undecided (27 per cent). This indicates that there are still many doubts amongst local authorities about the usefulness of the introductory tenancy. A number of matters clearly call to be considered before making the decision.

■ Given that a scheme will only apply to new tenants and that they will become secure after 12 months, what evidence is there that new tenants are causing anti-social behaviour in the first 12 months of their tenancy?

■ Will the requirements for internal appeal (see Chapter 3) make the scheme procedurally more cumbersome and difficult to operate than simply seeking possession in the normal way?

■ Do the legal uncertainties regarding whether decisions to evict can be challenged (see Chapter 3) provide sufficient uncertainty regarding the operation of the scheme to make it not viable to operate (at least at present until the legal position is clarified)?

There are no easy answers to these questions, and as yet no evidence to suggest what effect, if any, introductory tenancies will have on anti-social behaviour.

For registered social landlords, there is no statutory scheme equivalent to introductory tenancies. Some registered social landlords have adopted what effectively amounts to such a scheme by granting assured shorthold tenancies to new tenants, and only converting these to fully assured tenancies after the successful completion of the fixed term probationary period. While there are no direct legal controls over adopting such a policy, in practice registered social landlords need to comply with the guidance given by the Housing Corporation before granting shorthold tenancies rather than fully assured.

The Performance Standards for Registered Social Landlords (paras. G1.3 and F1.3), issued by the Corporation, give detailed guidance about when registered social landlords may adopt 'local lettings policies' that may include the use of assured shorthold tenancies.

Evidence gathering

While strengthening the tenancy agreement terms may assist in securing successful legal action, the experience of many social landlords is that it is only a first step and that it has to be combined with measures to improve the quality of evidence against perpetrators. These measures essentially fall into two categories:

1. *Confidence building amongst victims*: many cases fail because victims are unwilling to give evidence and most attempts to take legal action are likely to fail unless combined with measures to make the victims, the potential witnesses, confident enough to give evidence. These are considered further in Chapter 8.

2. *Use of professional or other third party witnesses*: some landlords have sought to improve the quality of evidence they are able to bring to court by using witnesses other than the victims. This may take the form of 'professional' witnesses (i.e. private detectives employed specifically for the evidence gathering task) or may be simply using the landlord's own staff. Some authorities have set up 'ranger' or 'security' forces to patrol estates (see further below) and the staff used in these schemes may be able to act as witnesses, particularly where they have been called to deal with particular incidents. The use of professional and other witnesses is discussed further in Chapter 8 below.

Monitoring

A number of social landlords now regularly monitor the views of their tenants in order to determine priorities and assess the effectiveness of existing policies. Where this is being undertaken, monitoring of policies to deal with anti-social behaviour can easily be incorporated. Monitoring can provide information on the problems which tenants are facing and whether strategies for dealing with them are effective.

A survey of tenant priorities carried out for the London Borough of Camden, for example, showed that 59 per cent of tenants who had reported an incident of anti-social behaviour were dissatisfied with the outcome, principally because no action was taken. This result indicates two potential problems: first, whether the council was responding appropriately to complaints; secondly, whether the council was failing to communicate to complainants what action had been taken. If no action was the appropriate response, for whatever reason, was this being properly explained to tenants? Once the problem has been identified, it is also important that a response is made. In the case of Camden, it is clear that they have sought to address the problem strategically by looking at their tenancy conditions and by setting up a particular effective working relationship with their lawyers (see below).

Mediation

As part of an overall strategy many landlords have sought to develop mediation services. The service can then be offered to tenants in appropriate circumstances. While some land-lords have established their own services in-house, many have found it more appropriate to seek to encourage (and fund) independent services that can be seen to be operating separately from the landlord. There is some debate about whether mediation is appropriate in all circumstances, or whether it is only appropriate in less serious cases of neigh-bour dispute. Nonetheless, mediation can provide an effec-tive means of resolving disputes between neighbours, and landlords should ensure that it is a service to which tenants have access.

Some work has been done in seeking to assess the effectiveness of mediation services (see Dignan, Sorsby and Hibbert, *Neighbourhood disputes: comparing the cost effectiveness of mediation and alternative approaches*, University of Sheffield, Centre for Criminological and Legal Research).

Ranger services

A number of local authorities have introduced some form of 'ranger' or 'security' services onto their estates in an effort to reduce anti-social behaviour. Such a service may provide a continual (and sometimes uniformed) presence on the estate, which may operate both to deter anti-social behaviour and also be called to deal with specific incidents that arise. One important consideration is how such a service will be paid for; generally such schemes are paid for by specific rent rises.

The nature of such a service also requires careful consideration, particularly to ensure that there is a proper division of responsibility between rangers and housing officers. If not, it is possible that tenants will be uncertain about where they must take their complaints. Social landlords will also want to consider carefully how far they wish to become responsible for what is effectively 'low level' policing of their estates and how far they wish to move towards an American model where housing authorities have their own police forces.

Another approach may be to seek additional assistance from the police themselves. As part of a package of measures (which included tenancy enforcement officers and community development workers to help tenants find jobs), Home Housing Association, paid Northumbria police for two full-time officers to work on one of their estates (*Inside Housing*, 20 December 1996: p. 5).

Training

A comprehensive policy cannot be expected to work unless the operational staff are adequately trained. The Chartered

Institute of Housing in its *Housing Management Standards Manual* suggests that training for housing staff in conciliation techniques, negotiation skills, legal remedies and the landlord's policy and procedures for dealing with nuisance and neighbour problems should be provided.

Inter-agency working

Anti-social behaviour is not a matter that landlords can deal with in isolation from other services. It requires a multi-agency approach. Within local authorities contacts must be maintained with environmental health, planning and social services. Environmental health departments can take action in relation to noise, rubbish and animals, and given their immediate powers (see Chapter 6) are very important in dealing with noise nuisance in particular. Planning departments can also make a contribution where, for example, tenants are using their homes to run a business. Where children or vulnerable adults are involved in nuisance behaviour, rather than punitive measures it may be that the support of social services is needed.

Outside the local authority, the main agency with which contact should be made is the police. In cases of serious criminal behaviour it is essential to liaise with the police. There are now examples of good co-operative working, which brings benefits to both the landlord and the police. Thus agreements with the police can lead to access to police information on successful criminal prosecutions. It has not been unusual for landlords only to find out about convictions haphazardly, for example through local newspaper reports. Proper exchange of information can mean that, where they may assist in securing evictions, convictions are automatically brought to the landlord's attention. Furthermore a good relationship may mean that police officers will attend civil courts to give evidence in eviction proceedings, even where no criminal proceedings are being contemplated. The new requirement to create a crime and disorder strategy (see above, p. 12) should also promote and enhance co-operative working with the police.

Problem estates

It is not unusual for particular estates to have problems over and above those encountered in a landlord's other properties. Such estates are generally characterised by serious criminal activity, particularly centred on drug dealing and by high void rates, as tenants seek to move out and offers on the estate are frequently rejected. In these circumstances a special strategy may need to be adopted to turn the estate around. This undoubtedly has to involve all agencies and the police. It may also require special policies, combining some or all of the strategies outlined above (e.g. on allocations, provision of youth services, physical alterations and employment measures) to be successful. Although such intensive work may be expensive in the short term, the long-term savings by way of lower void rates, for instance, may well mean it is worth while in economic as well as purely social terms.

An example of a successful estate strategy implemented on the Kingsmead Estate in the London Borough of Hackney is to be found in *Crime, Community and Change*, (NACRO, 1996). Another example, on a very local scale, comes from Denstone Crescent on the Fincham Estate in Knowsley. The road had become a haven for drug dealing, and more than a quarter of the 100 houses had become vacant and vandalised. In 1995 the council set up a working group of housing officers, police and residents to deal solely with these problems. A residents' association was set up, and was consulted extensively on the measures to be taken. Steps were taken to 'design' out crime, including splitting the road in two to create two cul-de-sacs. The police took special measures, with 28 arrests for drug possession being made in a two-week period. The residents' association has become involved in selecting new tenants. The result has been a transformation and earned Knowsley Borough Council the prize for best practice in housing management in the 1997 National Housing Awards (see report in *Inside Housing*, 10 October 1997: pp. 16-17).

Relationships with lawyers and courts

It is not uncommon to hear housing officers complaining that legal action is not taken because their solicitors have said that the case cannot go ahead. In order for effective legal action to take place there must be a good relationship between the housing officers and their solicitors. This requires both sides to know exactly what is required of them, and in particular for a clear agreement with the solicitors (be they in-house or external) as to time-scales for action. It is particularly important when using in-house solicitors that there is a designated solicitor within the legal department who is familiar with this type of work and able to give it proper priority. The advantages of a proper relationship are illustrated by the success achieved by the London Borough of Camden, where there is a dedicated housing team within the legal service's department. The team operates in the same way as a private firm, acting only on instructions and billing its clients (primarily the housing department) every month. The team issues progress reports every six weeks, and regular liaison meetings are held. Of the 40 cases referred to the team in 1996, 14 outright and three suspended possession orders were obtained (see further *Inside Housing* 3 October 1997: p. 25).

As well as a good relationship with the solicitors who will be conducting cases through the courts, landlords should consider their relationship with the court itself. If cases are failing at court it may be that the judges involved are not really aware of the seriousness of the problems being encountered by tenants. Although the climate does seem to be changing, with judges taking a very serious attitude to allegations of nuisance, this change can only be promoted further by making judges aware of the nature of the problems that tenants have to live with on a daily basis. Lord Woolf, in his report *Access to Justice* (Ch. 16, para. 40), suggested that those county court judges who specialise in housing cases 'should regard it as part of their duty to visit local council estates and hold structured discussions with tenants' representatives to give them a better understanding of the problems faced' in nuisance and harassment cases. This has already occurred in Leicester, where the City Council arranged for two of its local judges to meet tenants' groups.

Another forum for gaining access to judges and court officials is through county court user-groups and, if not already a member, it may be worthwhile seeking to join such a group, particularly if issues arise relating to court practices. Matters such as listing practices, which will enable court dates to be obtained quickly, can be discussed in this forum. Further guidance on building better relationships with the court is available in *Getting the Best out of the Courts System in Possession Cases*, which was issued to local authorities jointly by the Department of the Environment, Transport and the Regions, the Welsh Office, and the Lord Chancellor's Department.

2.
Landlords' Liability for Third Party Nuisance

Nuisance caused by building's structure /
Quiet enjoyment / Anti-social behaviour

This chapter looks at how far the landlord can be legally responsible for nuisance and annoyance to neighbours caused by its tenants.

Causing a nuisance (i.e. using property in such a way that it causes a disturbance to neighbours) is a tort and gives rise to a cause of action for which the neighbour may sue. The person who is normally liable for a nuisance is the wrongdoer (i.e. the person who is causing the nuisance). A landlord can be liable for nuisance caused by its tenant if the landlord requires a tenant to do the acts complained of (*Hilton & Another v James Smith & Sons (Norwood) Ltd* (1979)). This seems unlikely to arise in the case of tenants of social landlords.

The courts have generally been reluctant to make landlords responsible for the conduct of their tenants. A distinction has been drawn between nuisance resulting from the physical structure of the building (so that a nuisance may be caused by the ordinary user of the building) and a nuisance which is wholly due to anti-social behaviour by other residents. The general approach of the courts has been to hold the landlord liable in the former case and not in the latter.

In relation to both types of nuisance, there is an increasing number of cases in which the victims of anti-social

behaviour seek remedies (either damages or specific performance) against the landlord rather than against the
perpetrator of the nuisance. There is a number of reasons
for this. Where the nuisance is lack of sound insulation the
landlord is likely to have the resources and responsibility for
carrying out such works. In other cases where the remedy
sought is damages, actions are often taken against the landlord because the landlord has the financial resources to meet
judgment whereas the perpetrator may well be impecunious.
The landlord makes a much more attractive legal target than
the anti-social tenant.

Nuisance caused by building's structure

The landlord may be liable for a nuisance caused by tenants
when a property is let in such a condition that ordinary use
of it would cause a nuisance. This problem usually occurs in
flats, when for example, walking around or conversation in
the flat overhead causes such a disturbance that it amounts
to a nuisance.

Case report

Mr Sampson was the tenant of a flat on a lease
granted on 31 March 1978. The flat above him was
empty until 11 August 1978 when it was let to a
tenant. Conversion works had been carried out
between 1974 and 1978 and the flat above Mr
Sampson was converted in such a way that there
were French windows leading to a terrace roof
above Mr Sampson's flat. Ordinary use of the
terrace caused a nuisance. In 1979, Mr Hodson-
Pressinger bought the entire property from the
previous landlord. The Court of Appeal held that the
property was not fit to be used in the normal way
without interfering with the reasonable enjoyment
by Mr Sampson of his flat. Mr Hodson-Pressinger
was liable because he accepted assignment of the
reversion and was authorising the nuisance and in

> **breach of the covenant for quiet enjoyment.**
> *Sampson v Hodson-Pressinger* (1981)

Thus landlords will be liable for any nuisance which they authorise. In order to authorise it, they must know about the nuisance, although in some circumstances that knowledge is presumed. One question that has arisen recently is at what time must the nuisance or likely nuisance be known about. Is it when the property is converted or when it is let to the complainant?

> *Case report*
>
> In 1975 Camden Council converted a property into three flats. In 1992 the premises were let to Ms Baxter. In 1995, Ms Baxter brought proceedings against the council for damages for distress and inconvenience resulting from nuisance from the ordinary domestic activities carried out in the lower and upper flats, due to lack of insulation. The conversion satisfied the building requirements in force at the time of the works in 1975 but not those at the date of the proceedings (building regulations are not retrospective). The judge decided that whether the landlord had knowledge of the nuisance should be decided as in 1975, and consequently it was not liable.
>
> The Court of Appeal disagreed and held that the relevant time to consider whether Camden was aware of the nuisance was the time of the letting in 1992. The Court also held that the fact that the council was not in breach of the building regulations was not decisive of the issue and that it was not relevant that the council was not under any duty to improve the premises. Accordingly the case was remitted to the county court to decide whether the level of noise did in fact constitute a nuisance, and whether Camden knew or should have been presumed to know that it would amount to a nuisance when it let the property to Ms Baxter in 1992.
> *Baxter v Camden London Borough Council* (1997)

The extent of a landlord's liability for nuisance resulting from structural problems will depend on the facts of each case; it is interesting to note that the judge who heard the second trial in *Baxter v Camden* held that the council was not liable.

Quiet enjoyment

An alternative argument to liability in nuisance is that the landlord is in breach of the tenant's right to quiet enjoyment. In *Baxter v Camden* (above) the Court of Appeal found that there could be a breach of the implied covenant for quiet enjoyment if the contemplated use for which the landlord let the adjoining flat was one which interfered with the reasonable enjoyment of the tenant's own flat. However, the argument was rejected in the case of *Southwark v Mills* (1998).

Case report

A number of tenants in a block owned by **Southwark London Borough Council** took action against the council on the basis that the properties were not adequately soundproofed and they could hear everything from the neighbouring flats. Under the terms of their tenancy agreements they could take disputes arising under the tenancy agreement to an arbitration tribunal. They took their claims to the tribunal on the basis that the lack of sound-proofing amounted to a breach of the implied term as to quiet enjoyment. The tribunal found for the tenants and ordered that sound-proofing should be carried out. The council appealed.

The Court of Appeal found that the council had not 'interrupted' or 'interfered with' the tenant's quiet enjoyment. The tenants were getting what they contracted for, i.e. a poorly sound-insulated flat. The Court recognised that there were now differing decisions about liability of landlords and gave leave to appeal to the House of Lords.

Southwark London Borough Council v Mills (1998)

Anti-social behaviour

Where action is being considered against a landlord in respect of anti-social behaviour by tenants (as opposed to nuisance caused by ordinary user) victims have sought redress, not just by actions in nuisance, but under four potential causes of action. These are:

■ nuisance
■ negligence
■ breach of contract
■ breach of statutory duty.

Actions by non-tenants

A landlord is not liable where someone who has entered the landlord's premises without permission acts in an objectionable way. Thus where a nuisance is caused by squatters (*Lamb v Camden London Borough Council* (1981)), trespassers (*King v Liverpool City Council* (1986)) or vandals (*Smith v Littlewoods Organisation Ltd* (1987)), the victims are unable to claim against the landlord. In *Page Motors Ltd v Epsom and Ewell Borough Council* (1981), however, the Court of Appeal did find a local authority liable for the nuisance caused by trespassing gypsies where they failed to take any action for five years (see further below).

Nuisance

Whether a landlord could be liable for the nuisance of its tenants has been considered in a number of cases. It is established that no claim can be sustained in nuisance where nuisance is caused by an extraordinary use of premises, such as the actions of other tenants or occupiers. The rationale behind this view is that it is up to the victim of the nuisance to take action against the perpetrator.

Case report

The London Borough of Lewisham was in the process of acquiring houses in a street for demolition and reconstruction. In the meantime it was using the houses it had acquired to accommodate the homeless. The authority housed a family (the Scotts), who it knew were likely to cause a nuisance, next to the house owned and lived in by Mr Smith. The tenancy agreement signed by the Scotts prohibited nuisance. Damage and noise nuisance from the family led to Mr Smith and his wife leaving their home and Mr Smith brought an action against the authority for an injunction restraining it from allowing those in the house adjoining him from causing a nuisance. It was held that the authority was not liable for the nuisance caused by the tenants because it had neither expressly nor impliedly authorised the nuisance.

Smith v Scott and others (1973)

The Court of Appeal has recently decided that this judgment is still good law.

Case report

Mr Hussain and Ms Livingstone were the joint owners of a shop with a flat above, which was situated in a housing estate owned by Lancaster City Council. There was considerable harassment of the couple, including threats and racist abuse. The couple sought damages from the council and an injunction requiring it to take reasonable steps to ensure that the nuisance ceased. The council sought to have the action struck out as disclosing no reasonable cause of action. The judge at first instance refused to do so, but the Court of Appeal allowed the council's appeal and struck the claim out.

A number of legal claims were made against the council. The first was that Lancaster was liable for the nuisance of the tenants. This was rejected on two grounds. First, no nuisance, in the technical

tortious sense, by the tenants or their families had been disclosed. Although the conduct clearly interfered with the couple's enjoyment of their land, it did not involve the tenants' use of the tenants' land, and thus was not a nuisance. Secondly, as to the ambit of the landlord's liability for nuisance, the Court of Appeal affirmed the decision in *Smith v Scott* (above).
Hussain and Livingstone v Lancaster City Council (1998)

There are some instances where a landlord has been held liable, e.g. where the landlord had a special role in managing a shopping mall (*Chartered Trust plc v Davies* (1997)). Liability was also found in the case of *Page Motors v Epsom & Ewell Borough Council* (1981).

Case report

Page Motors Ltd was a company that took a lease for occupation of part of an estate owned by the borough council. There were a number of gypsies living on the estate but the number increased rapidly. The gypsies burned rubbish and rubber causing acrid smoke; they obstructed the access to the premises; their dogs attacked customers and those who were delivering goods to the company. The result was a drop in the turnover of the business. The company made frequent complaints to the council, which then obtained an order for possession against the gypsies. The county council and later the then Department of the Environment persuaded the borough council not to enforce the order as to do so would be to transfer the problem elsewhere. The company brought an action for nuisance and the decision of the trial judge, that the council had adopted and continued the nuisance, was supported by the Court of Appeal. It is significant that the council used the unsupervised site to contain the borough's gypsy problem while policy decisions were made and that the council provided water, skips for refuse and facilities for sewage disposal.
Page Motors Ltd v Epsom and Ewell Borough Council (1981)

Page Motors was distinguished in the *Hussain* case on the basis that the conduct of the gypsies constituted a nuisance in the technical sense, involving misuse of the council's land by the gypsies, who had been occupying the land for several years.

Negligence

To found an action in negligence, any victim must show that there has been a breach of a duty of care owed by the alleged perpetrator. *Smith v Scott* (above) is also authority for the proposition that a landowner does not owe a duty of care to his or her neighbours when selecting tenants. The Court of Appeal followed this view in *O'Leary v London Borough of Islington* (1983) and also in *Hussain v Lancaster City Council* (above).

> ### Case report
>
> Tenancy agreements for tenants in a block of flats let by the London Borough of Islington stated: 'the tenant must not damage council property or cause your neighbours nuisance or annoyance or let your family or lodgers or visitors disturb them. This applies to common areas such as passages stairways and lifts and to estate grounds.' The second sentence was phrased as being without prejudice to the generality of the first. The O'Leary's were victims of nuisance caused by their neighbour. They took proceedings to compel the council to enforce the clause on the basis that there was an implied clause in their own tenancy that the landlord would enforce the clause in other agreements. They alleged the council was negligent for not having done so. The Court of Appeal held that there was no implied term and no duty of care and that the council was therefore not liable.
>
> *O'Leary v London Borough of Islington* (1983)

Breach of contract

A term for enforcing nuisance clauses cannot be implied into a tenancy agreement (*O'Leary v London Borough of Islington,* above). The Court of Appeal decided that the plaintiff should have sought a remedy against the perpetrator of the nuisance and so there was no need to imply such a term. This view is based on basic principles of contract: a term will only be implied because of necessity and will not be implied if it would be inconsistent with the express wording of the contract.

The situation is more difficult in cases where there is an express term in the tenancy agreement for example, obliging a landlord to 'take all reasonable steps to prevent any nuisance.' However, even in such cases the courts have been reluctant to find that the landlord has been in breach of such a term (see *Helsdon v Camden London Borough Council* (1997) below).

Breach of statutory duty (local authorities)

Local authorities are in a particularly difficult position as there are occasions when their obligations as landlords can conflict with statutory obligations. Thus their requirement to fulfil statutory obligations (e.g. towards the homeless or under community care legislation) is a factor which, in the public interest, should be taken into account in claims for nuisance, negligence or breach of contract, which puts them on a different footing from private landlords. On the other hand their specific duties may require them to take action to prevent anti-social behaviour, and leave them open to a claim should they fail to do so. The most obvious statutory duty in this regard lies under the Race Relations Act (RRA) 1976 (see p. 33 below).

The obligations of local authorities in respect of breach of statutory duties were considered in *X (Minors) v Bedfordshire County Council* (1995) where Lord Browne-Wilkinson stated:

> "...to found a cause of action flowing from the care-
> less exercise of statutory duties the plaintiff has to
> show that the circumstances are such as to raise a
> duty of care at common law." ... "The local authority
> cannot be liable for doing that which Parliament has
> authorised..." unless "the decision complained of is
> so unreasonable that it falls outside the ambit of such
> statutory discretion."

This decision has made it very difficult to take action
on the basis of breach of statutory duty, as has been illustrated in the area of anti-social behaviour by the case of
Hussain v Lancaster City Council (above). The Court of Appeal
in that case rejected a claim based on negligence in the
exercise of statutory powers.

The vulnerable

Local authorities are under an obligation to house those who
are in priority need (section 59(1) of HA 1985) the definition
of which includes those who are vulnerable (section 59(1)(c)).
The result is that there is an increasing problem whereby
those who are vulnerable are housed next to other tenants
and cause those tenants to suffer a nuisance.

The implications of policies such as care in the
community, particularly when coupled with a reduction in
housing stock due to the Right to Buy policy has increased
the problem. Local authorities frequently have to balance
the needs of vulnerable tenants against the needs of other
neighbouring tenants.

Case report

Mrs Helsdon sought to recover damages against the
council resulting from nuisance caused by vulnerable
tenants who were housed by the council in flats near to
her home. A clause in the tenancy agreement stated
the council would use its best endeavours to prevent
nuisance on any part of the estate. At court Mrs

> Helsdon argued that due to their mental incapacity no remedy was available against the perpetrators of the nuisance. It was said that the landlord was liable for nuisance resulting from its housing those individuals, because at the time of allocation the council knew that they were likely to cause a nuisance. The council was also liable because no remedy by way of injunction would be available and because it had failed to take action, specifically proceedings for possession. Mrs Helsdon relied on *Wookey v Wookey* (1991) (see p. 84, below) and the express terms of the contract.
>
> The argument was rejected not least on the basis that Mrs Helsdon had herself obtained an injunction against the perpetrators of the nuisance. Furthermore, a claim on the basis that possession proceedings should have been taken was asking the court to adjudicate on the prospects of success of a claim that had never been brought involving potential defendants who had not given evidence in the case. As such it was too remote. The judge held that it could not be in the public interest to oblige a local authority to take possession proceedings and to do so would be to interfere with matters that were within the council's discretion.
>
> *Helsdon v London Borough of Camden* (1997)

The above case demonstrates the reluctance of the courts to find a landlord liable, even in the most extreme case and in one where an express term of the contract provides that the landlord would use its best endeavours to prevent a nuisance. Significantly, the perpetrators were so vulnerable that the council may have had a responsibility to re-house them even if they had been evicted.

Obligations under Race Relations Act

Section 21(2) of the RRA 1976 provides:

> "(2) It is unlawful for a person, in relation to premises managed by him to discriminate against a person occupying the premises –

(b) by evicting him or subjecting him to any other detriment."

Discrimination is defined in section 1(1)(a) of RRA 1976 as treating a person less favourably than they would treat others, on racial grounds.

Section 71 of RRA 1976 imposes a general duty on local authorities to ensure that their functions are carried out with regard to the need to eliminate unlawful racial discrimination. Can the failure to prevent racial harassment amount to a breach of this statutory duty?

Case report

Mr and Mrs El-Sammadoni claimed damages against the London Borough of Camden alleging that the council had failed to take action to stop racial taunts and nuisance such as ringing on their doorbell by the children of neighbours. The court rejected their argument that they were entitled to damages because the council had failed to take possession proceedings against the alleged perpetrators. The council had carried out an extensive investigation and although it accepted that there was evidence of harassment it concluded that it was not racial in nature. The court was being asked to award damages for the possibility of success in possession proceedings, actions that were never brought, and the claim was too remote. However, it was considered that there was a possibility of recovery under these sections of the Race Relations Act in principle.
El-Sammadoni v Camden London Borough Council (1997)

In summary the position is as follows:

1. under section 21(2) of RRA 1976 landlords are liable if they discriminate against tenants or subject them to a detriment such as racial harassment;
2. it is unlikely that landlords will be liable under section 21(2), for racial harassment caused to their tenants by third parties (although there is no binding authority on the point);

3. in principle local authorities may be liable for damages under section 71 RRA 1976, if it can be shown that they failed to comply with their general duty to ensure that their functions are carried out with regard to the need to eliminate unlawful racial discrimination (again there is no authority on this point).

However, it is expected that the reluctance demonstrated by the courts to find local authorities liable for anti-social acts of third parties in respect of other causes of action is likely to be followed in claims under this head. The evidence in such cases would have to be overwhelming.

3.

Introductory Tenancies

Aim of introductory tenancies /
Electing to operate scheme / Duration /
Cessation of introductory tenancy / Possession /
Review / Challenges to eviction decision /
Rights of introductory tenants

Aim of introductory tenancies

The most innovative provision dealing with anti-social behaviour contained in the Housing Act 1996 was the 'introductory tenancy'. This new type of tenancy aims to address the particular problem faced by housing authorities when secure tenancies have been granted to tenants who subsequently cause a nuisance. The disruption caused by such tenants (and often, whole families) can change the nature of entire estates and undermine plans to improve community spirit and morale.

The difficulty that often faces housing authorities is the time that it takes to secure an order for possession. Frequently witnesses are reluctant to give evidence, particularly in the most serious cases. In order to satisfy the criteria of the Housing Act 1985 it is necessary to satisfy a court that it is reasonable to grant an order for possession (see Chapter 4 below). This means that there can be no guarantee of success in an action against a secure tenant.

Introductory tenancies are a mechanism whereby local housing authorities can monitor the first year of a tenancy and if it is not satisfactory, due to anti-social behaviour, seek possession unfettered by the above considerations. Often those who cause nuisance do so from the commencement of the tenancy, yet are treated in the same way as those who have been satisfactory tenants for years; the scheme directly addresses this problem. In Chapter 1 we looked at some of the considerations which go into deciding whether to operate the system. In this chapter we examine the details of the scheme.

Electing to operate the scheme

Section 124(1) of HA 1996 provides that a local housing authority or housing action trust may elect to operate an introductory tenancy regime. By section 124(2), once the authority or trust has elected to operate the scheme all new tenancies that would otherwise be secure are, with some exceptions, treated as introductory tenancies. The scheme also applies to licences which would otherwise be secure (section 126 of HA 1996, and see A. Dymond, *Security of Tenure* (Arden's Housing Library) 1995: Ch. 2).

The exceptions are that the tenant, or in the case of joint tenants at least one of them was:

1. already a secure tenant of the same or another dwelling house, e.g. where the tenant is transferred due to major refurbishment works;
2. an assured tenant of a registered social landlord (otherwise than under an assured shorthold tenancy) in respect of the same or another dwelling house, e.g. on a mutual exchange between a local authority and a housing association tenant.

The authority has to elect to operate the scheme in respect of *all* new tenancies and cannot be selective. If the authority chooses not to operate the scheme then it cannot create any introductory tenancies. However, by virtue of section 124(5) of HA 1996, the authority is not prevented from electing to operate the scheme at a later date; if it does so it then applies to all new tenancies, apart from the exceptions outlined above.

The scheme does not apply to tenancies that already exist. It will not, therefore, assist housing authorities in respect of tenants who hold existing secure tenancies; in such cases it will be necessary to establish that there are grounds for possession pursuant to Schedule 2 to HA 1985 (see Chapter 4 below).

Duration

By section 125(1) a tenancy remains an introductory tenancy until the end of the trial period, namely one year from the start of the period (section 125(2)). The trial period commences on the date on which the local housing authority or housing action trust enters into the tenancy or, if later, the date on which the tenant is first entitled to possession. This covers with the situation that commonly occurs where tenancy agreements are signed on a date prior to the tenancy start date (e.g. where works need to be completed to the property).

Adoption of tenancies

A new landlord can adopt tenancies. This occurs where an authority or trust becomes a landlord under the tenancy as a result of the disposal or surrender of the former landlord's interest (section 124(4) of HA 1996). Typically this takes place where properties are transferred between authorities or from a housing association to an authority. If the tenancy has been adopted the trial period starts on the date of adoption (section 125(2)(b)), subject to certain exceptions set out in section 125(3).

These exceptions deal with the situation where there was an introductory tenancy or an equivalent in existence prior to the transfer. Thus, if the tenant in such a case was formerly a tenant under another introductory tenancy (or held an assured shorthold tenancy from a registered social landlord), time as an introductory (or shorthold) tenant counts towards the trial period. This rule is subject to the proviso that the tenancy must have ended immediately before the trial period and, in the case of more than one such tenancy, that they succeeded each other without interruption.

Cessation of introductory tenancy

The introductory nature of tenancy may cease in a number of circumstances set out in section 125(5) of HA 1996.

Tenancy not otherwise secure

The introductory tenancy is only designed to apply to tenancies that would otherwise be secure. Thus if the tenancy would not otherwise be a secure tenancy, for example if the tenant is no longer using the property as his or her only or principal home (see A Dymond, *Security of Tenure* (Arden's Housing Library) 1995: Ch. 4), it also ceases to be introductory. In these circumstances the tenant ceases to have any statutory security of tenure and becomes a non-secure tenant.

Other landlords

If the property is transferred to a landlord who is not a local housing authority or housing action trust, the tenancy ceases to be introductory and becomes subject to the statutory regime of the new landlord.

Revocation

The authority or trust may decide to revoke the scheme, in which case, assuming all the necessary conditions continue to apply, all tenancies become secure.

Succession

If section 133(3) of HA 1996 relating to succession applies (see p. 47 below), the tenancy ceases to be introductory and ceases to have any security of tenure.

Possession

Unlike a secure tenancy where possession for anti-social behaviour is at the discretion of the court (see p. 69 below), provided the landlord has complied with all the procedural requirements, the court *must* grant possession of an introductory tenancy when sought by the landlord.

Notice

Before seeking possession the landlord is required to serve a notice of proceedings for possession (section 127(2) of HA 1996). Unlike secure tenancies there is no prescribed form for the notice; however, it must comply with the following (section 128):

1. It must state that the court will be asked to make an order for possession of a dwelling house.
2. The notice must give the landlord's reasons for applying for the order.
3. It must specify a date after which proceedings for possession may be begun (this cannot be earlier than the tenancy could be terminated by a notice to quit, generally four weeks, see A. Dymond, *Security of Tenure* (Arden's Housing Library) 1995: Ch. 5). The court cannot entertain proceedings brought prior to this date.
4. The notice must state that the tenant has the right to request a review of the decision to take proceedings for possession and must give the time limit (14 days).
5. The notice must notify the tenant that advice should be sought from a Citizens Advice Bureau, a housing aid

centre, a law centre, or a solicitor immediately if it is required.

Reasons

While the notice must state the reasons for seeking possession the Housing Act 1996 gives no indication of what these reasons may encompass. Clearly anti-social behaviour provides an adequate reason. DETR Circular 2/97 (Part V of HA 1996 – Conduct of Tenants: Introductory Tenancies and Repossession for Secure Tenancies) states (at paragraph 19): it 'is envisaged that the majority of possession cases will relate to persistent anti-social behaviour or rent arrears'. What is less clear is whether other grounds, (e.g. under-occupation, or a need to carry out major works) would provide an adequate reason. There is nothing in the wording of the statute to suggest any limitation providing the landlord is acting in good faith and it is difficult to envisage any basis for challenging such a decision (see further p. 46 below on challenging decisions to evict).

It has been said in relation to statutory duties to give reasons in other contexts that reasons should be 'proper, intelligible and adequate'. DETR Circular 2/97 suggests (at paragraph 16) that 'as good practice landlords should include a full statement of the reasons for seeking possession, which could include a case history of the sequence of events'. The former would seem to be a necessary requirement to comply with the law, and failure to do so could leave landlords open to challenge (see p. 46 below). The Circular continues:

> "The statement should contain as much information as possible to enable the tenant to prepare his case should he take up his right to a review. It should not contain information which could lead to witness intimidation (such as names and addresses)."

Court

The landlord can only gain possession of an introductory tenancy by order of the court (section 127(1) of HA 1996). A summons for possession must, accordingly, be issued and the necessary evidence presented to the court at the hearing. Because the court has no discretion but to grant possession, any order will have to be outright.

The court does not have the jurisdiction to grant suspended orders. This leaves authorities and trusts in some difficulty if the reason for seeking possession is, for example, rent arrears, and they would not normally seek an outright order. DETR Circular 2/97 suggests (at paragraph 20) that landlords may wish to devise their own procedures (such as the collection of rent plus arrears by instalment) for introductory tenants to replace the use of suspended possession orders. While this may prove effective in some cases, in many it is only by going to court that the necessary payments can be extracted. If landlords choose to let tenants remain after an outright possession order has been made, they need to be very careful that they do not unintentionally create a new tenancy (see generally, *Burrows v Brent London Borough Council* (1997)).

The tenancy ends on the date on which the tenant is to give up possession pursuant to the court order (section 127(3) of HA 1996). Section 89 of HA 1980 applies and the court is able to postpone possession for up to 14 days or, in cases of exceptional hardship, six weeks.

Review

The tenant may seek a review of the decision to take proceedings for possession under section 129. The tenant must make a request for such review within 14 days from the date of service of the notice. The landlord must then review, and notify the tenant of, the decision and, if the original decision is upheld, the reasons why this is the case. The review must be carried out and notification given before the date after which proceedings for possession may be begun as set out in the notice. For this reason, although the usual requirement is for the notice to be four weeks (see above), landlords may wish to consider giving a longer period in order that they do not have to carry out the review in a very constrained time-frame.

Procedure on review

Regulations may be made by the Secretary of State on the procedure to be followed for review. The Introductory Tenants (Review) Regulations 1997 ('the Regulations') (SI 1997 No. 72) provide:

1. the review will not be by way of oral hearing unless the tenant informs the landlord that he or she wishes to have such a hearing within the 14-day time limit;
2. the review must be carried out by someone who was not involved in the decision to apply for possession;
3. there are no limitations on who that person can be (it does not have to be an officer and could, for example, be a panel of councillors), but if it is an officer, the officer must be senior to the original decision-maker; and
4. if there is not to be a hearing the tenant may make representations in writing. The landlord is obliged to consider such representations and to inform the tenant of the date by which the representations are to be received (this cannot be earlier that five clear days of the receipt of this information by the tenant).

Oral hearings

The actual procedure at any oral hearing is a matter for the person conducting the review except that the Regulations provide that:

1. the tenant has the right to be accompanied to the hearing and/or be represented by another person (who need not be professionally qualified); and
2. the tenant or representative may call witnesses, question any witness and make written representations.

There is no right to 'call' witnesses (i.e. they cannot be forced to attend). The DETR Circular states (at paragraph 23) that the case for the local authority 'may be presented by a housing officer who can use hearsay evidence and who will not have to identify who made the complaints.' While this may be true in some cases, it must be remembered that the conduct of the review must satisfy the requirements of administrative law (see p. 46 below) and be fair, so that a tenant must be given the opportunity to answer properly the allegations against him or her.

Absences and adjournments

The Regulations provide that:
1. the landlord is obliged to give the tenant notice of the date, time and place of the hearing and the hearing should be not less than five days after the receipt of a request for a hearing. The hearing cannot proceed if the requisite notice has not been given unless the tenant or the tenant's representative consents;
2. if the tenant fails to appear (notice having been given) the person conducting the review may proceed (having regard to all the circumstances including any explanation offered for the absence) or give directions regarding the conduct of the review as they think fit;
3. the tenant may ask for the landlord to postpone the hearing and the landlord may grant or refuse the application as they see fit;
4. the person hearing the review has wide powers to adjourn the review at any stage. However, if the matter is adjourned part-heard and the composition of

those hearing the review varies, a complete rehearing of the case is required; and

5. if more than one person is conducting the review, providing the tenant or their representative consents, the hearing can proceed in the absence of one of the persons that is to determine the review.

Where hearings are postponed or adjourned it must be remembered that they still need to be completed within the notice period.

Effect of beginning proceedings for possession

It may be the case that the landlord commences possession proceedings prior to the end of the trial period, but that the court does not decide them within the period. In this case the tenancy does not automatically become secure at the end of the period; instead, by section 130(1) and (2) of HA 1996 the introductory nature of the tenancy continues until the court orders possession. Similarly, if the tenancy ceases to fulfil the requirements for a secure tenancy, and thus also ceases to be introductory after possession proceedings are commenced, the tenancy is continued as an introductory tenancy until the possession proceedings are determined.

Where the tenancy ceases to be introductory because of a change of landlord, revocation of the scheme or because there is no one entitled to succeed (see pp. 38-39 above), the tenancy ceases to be introductory but the landlord (or on transfer the new landlord) may continue the proceedings, and the provisions for possession continue to apply as if the tenancy had remained introductory (section 130(3)). Where in such a case a tenant would otherwise become secure (e.g. because of revocation of the scheme) he or she does not become entitled to exercise the right to buy until the court decides that he or she is not required to give possession (section 130(4)).

Challenges to eviction decision

Although there is no statutory defence to any action brought provided the correct procedural steps have been taken, this is not to say that there can be no legal challenge to the decision to evict. The decision to evict can be challenged on administrative (i.e. public) law principles. (This is clear from cases decided prior to local authority tenants becoming secure in 1980: see *Bristol District Council v Clark* (1975) and *Cannock Chase District Council v Kelly* (1978)). Thus, for example, if the landlord has not acted in good faith, or has not acted fairly, or has taken irrelevant considerations into account, it could be challenged. It is clear from the cases, however, that the burden lies on the tenant to show that there has been a public law failure in this respect. The duty to give reasons may, though, make it easier to show that the landlord has not acted properly, and make it more likely that a challenge will be successful than was the case prior to 1980.

Normally where a public law challenge is mounted to a decision of a local authority, proceedings have to be taken by way of judicial review in the High Court. Thus there is a maximum three-month time limit, and leave to proceed has to be sought. Where, however, the public law challenge provides a defence to possession proceedings there is an exception to this rule. In *Wandsworth London Borough Council v Winder* (1985), the House of Lords permitted a secure tenant to resist proceedings for possession based on arrears of rent where the challenge was that an increase in the arrears was unlawful on public law grounds. It seems likely that this principle would also apply to introductory tenancies so that a tenant could raise the public law defence in the county court action for possession.

Rights of introductory tenants

An introductory tenant does not have the same rights as a secure tenant. For example, an introductory tenant cannot sub-let or exercise the right to buy (see C. Hunter, *Tenants' Rights* (Arden's Housing Library) 1995 and J. Henderson, *Rights to Buy and Acquire* (Arden's Housing Library) 1997) but the Housing Act 1996 does make provision for succession to and assignment of introductory tenancies.

Succession

It is possible to succeed to an introductory tenancy (section 133 of HA 1996). The provisions are comparable with those relating to secure tenancies. A person can succeed to the introductory tenancy upon the tenant's death if he or she is the spouse or another member of the tenant's family who has resided with the tenant for the 12 months prior to his or her death. These provisions are not applicable if the tenant was a successor (see C. Hunter, *Tenants' Rights* (Arden's Housing Library) 1995: Ch. 2). Where there is no one entitled to succeed, the tenancy generally ceases to be introductory (section 133(3)).

Assignment

By section 134 the only circumstances in which an introductory tenancy can be assigned are:
1. pursuant to orders relating either to section 24 of the Matrimonial Causes Act 1973, section 17(1) of the Matrimonial and Family Proceedings Act 1984 or paragraph 1 of Schedule 1 to the Children Act 1989, or
2. an assignment to a person who would be entitled to succeed the tenancy had the tenant died immediately before the assignment. These are the same as for secure tenants (see C. Hunter, *Tenants' Rights*, above).

Conclusion

Introductory tenancies provide housing authorities with the potential to address anti-social behaviour by tenants with speed and unhampered by a dependence upon other tenants acting as witnesses. A potential drawback to the scheme is the possibility of proceedings being taken following unsubstantiated allegations that cannot be challenged by the tenant's representatives under cross-examination. A further difficulty is the requirement that the authorities are required to opt into the whole scheme. There is also some uncertainty over whether, and if with any success, the decision to evict can be challenged in the courts. The benefits of the scheme cannot be measured until it is known how many authorities have adopted the scheme and it has been tested in practice.

4.

Nuisance Behaviour by Tenants

Terms of tenancy / Injunctions and causes
of action / Types of injunction: final and
interlocutory / Terms of injunction /
Powers of arrest / Effect of breach of injunction /
Anti-social behaviour orders / Grounds for
possession / Procedure for obtaining possession /
Reasonable to continue to occupy

The two main remedies available to landlords to deal with
anti-social behaviour by tenants are possession and injunction.
The two are not mutually exclusive and landlords may want
to seek an injunction first and then move on to possession.

Terms of tenancy

Whether an injunction or possession is sought, the terms of the
tenancy are important. If an injunction is sought it is generally
on the basis of breach of terms of the tenancy. If possession is
sought it may well be under Ground of 1 HA 1985 or Ground
12 of HA 1988 (i.e. breach of terms of the tenancy).

Most landlords seem to have their own terms. Some
can be very brief: for example, 'The tenant shall not be
a nuisance and annoyance to neighbours.' This is not
adequate, and it is much more effective to have a more ex-

tensive clause that spells out clearly what is expected of the tenant. The clause should:

■ Define who is to be protected by the term 'neighbours'. How wide a geographical area is to be included? Should it be extended beyond the usual, relatively small area encapsulated by the term 'neighbours' or indeed now the wider concept of 'locality'. Should it include the landlord's staff and other workers who may be abused?

■ Be more explicit about what is meant by nuisance and annoyance. It is helpful to list as examples (without prejudice to other instances) the types of behaviour that will not be tolerated and may include violence, threats of violence, and other verbal abuse.

Specific terms will be considered in Chapter 6.

Injunctions and causes of action

An injunction is an order of the court requiring a person to do or refrain from doing a particular act. In cases of anti-social behaviour by the tenant the order will usually require that he or she refrains from acting in a particular way.

In order to obtain an injunction the applicant must have a 'cause of action'. The most usual cause is breach of the tenancy agreement (i.e. a breach of contract). Where the landlord's property is also being damaged by the tenant's conduct, the landlord can sue on the basis of the tort of nuisance. However, in general the law of nuisance does not provide a cause of action where it is other residents who are suffering from the behaviour, since the landlord is not directly affected by the action. Thus, for example, noise nuisance affects the neighbours, but does not affect the value of the landlord's property, and accordingly any injunction would have to be based on a breach of tenancy and not the tort of nuisance. The Housing Act 1996, also introduces a new statutory cause of action (see further below).

Breach of terms of the tenancy

Where action is being taken against the tenant the most obvious cause of action is breach of the terms of the tenancy. Thus where the tenancy sets out a particular course of action which the tenant must not undertake, an injunction can be sought to prevent the tenant acting in breach of that term (e.g. regarding the making of noise nuisance, or the keeping of pets).

Housing Act 1996

The HA 1996 introduced a new statutory basis for all local authorities to obtain injunctions; the provisions are applicable to both tenants and non-tenants. The injunction may only be granted if:

1. the person against whom it is sought has used or threatened violence against a person residing in, visiting or otherwise engaging in lawful activity in any local authority dwelling houses held under secure or introductory tenancies, or other accommodation provided by the authority in discharging its duty towards the homeless or in the locality of such premises; and
2. there is a significant risk of harm to that or any other such person if the injunction is not granted.

Such injunctions are really aimed at severe cases of actual or threatened violence, and cannot be used for other types of nuisance such as noise, or indeed other criminal activities such as drug dealing if there has been no element of violence involved.

Other provisions

In addition to breach of contract and the HA 1996, landlords have sought injunctions on the basis of other causes of action. As has already been stated, it is often difficult for a landlord to show that there is an action in nuisance, but this may sometimes be applicable. Another basis that can be used is trespass (where e.g. the tenant is using empty property from which to cause a nuisance). Local authorities have also used their powers under section 222 of the Local Government Act (LGA) 1972, and the fall-back powers in section 111 of LGA 1972 allied to their powers to manage their properties under Part II of HA 1985.

Where it is the tenant who is causing the nuisance, however, the simplest and most straightforward action is that of breach of tenancy. If there is a properly drawn up tenancy agreement, there should be no need to have recourse to any of these actions. They are, however, considered in more detail in relation to nuisance by non-tenants in Chapter 5 below.

Environmental Protection Act 1990

One other possible cause of action will arise where the conduct amounts to a statutory nuisance under the Environmental Protection Act 1990 (see p. 103, below). Where the authority is of the opinion that criminal proceedings would be an inadequate remedy, the authority may take injunction proceedings in the High Court under section 81(5) of EPA 1990. Such proceedings must be taken against the 'person responsible' for the nuisance which may be the tenant or someone else living at the property.

This may be an appropriate remedy in cases e.g. of noise nuisance, where the tenant fails to respond to an abatement notice, and the criminal proceedings may take some time to be heard.

Types of injunction: final and interlocutory

Injunctions can be *final* (i.e. part of the decision of the court after all matters have been heard at trial) or *interlocutory* (interim) (i.e. made at an early point in the case before all matters have been heard). In practice their greatest use is at the interim stage, providing an immediate remedy.

Procedure and evidence

The application begins by lodging the necessary papers with the court. These include the particulars of claim (which set out the cause of action and case against the defendant), affidavits giving the factual evidence relied upon, and a draft of the injunction sought. Unless the application is made *ex parte* (see below), the applicant is always required to give the defendant two clear days' notice of an application for an injunction. Once the papers are lodged, a date will be set for the hearing, which gives time for the defendant to be served with copies.

The hearing takes place on the basis of the affidavit evidence that the court has, and it is therefore vital that this is well presented. It should, if possible, include direct evidence of the behaviour that is being complained about. One advantage of interlocutory hearings, however, is that the court can accept affidavits which contain hearsay evidence (see RSC Order 41, rule 5, applied to county courts by CCR Order 30, rule 10). The rules state that in interlocutory proceedings an affidavit 'may contain statements of information or belief with the sources and grounds thereof'. This means that a housing officer can give evidence that he or she was told of events by a tenant. The source of the information, however, must be identified. While this avoids tenants having to attend court and give evidence directly in any form, it cannot avoid altogether identifying those who have come forward to the landlord to complain.

The judge also has to be satisfied that there is a 'serious issue to be tried' (see below); the more indirect the evidence, the less likely it is that the judge will be so satisfied.

Ex parte applications

In urgent cases (e.g. where there has been violent behaviour) it is possible to apply *ex parte* (i.e. without giving the defendant notice of the proceedings). Specific provision is made for an *ex parte* application under section 152(7) of HA 1996 and the court may, under that subsection, grant an *ex parte* order where it considers it 'just and convenient to do so'. This is appropriate where, for example, notice of the proceedings might provoke the very harm it sought to avert.

Subsection (7) continues that where such an order is made the court 'must afford the respondent an opportunity to make representations relating to the injunction . . . as soon as just and convenient at a hearing of which notice has been given to all the parties . . .'. The provisions of subsection (7) reflect the usual practice of the courts in *ex parte* applications, as they would also be applied in applications relating to breach of the tenancy. This does not mean that there must be a hearing with all the parties after the *ex parte* order is made. The usual practice is to make an *ex parte* order with liberty for either side to apply to the court for a hearing to take place and this will be sufficient to comply with the requirements. Thus if the respondent tenant does not wish to contest the order there will be no need for any further hearing.

Basis for making an interim injunction

To obtain an interim injunction it is not necessary to prove the entire case. What must be shown is that 'there is a serious issue to be tried' and that the 'balance of convenience' lies in granting the injunction (see *American Cyanamid v Ethicon Ltd.* (1975)). Where all that is being sought is an order that the tenancy is complied with (e.g. by the tenant refraining from making unreasonable noise), the balance of convenience almost always lies in granting the injunction. After all, all that the tenant is being asked to do is to comply with the terms of the tenancy to which he or she has already agreed. Provided that there is some factual evidence of the breach in the affidavits, the court should exercise its discretion to grant the injunction.

Undertakings in damages

Where an interim injunction is sought it is usual for the applicant landlord to have to give an undertaking in damages to the respondent. This is activated if, at the final hearing, the judge decides the case in favour of the respondent tenant and concludes that the injunction should not have been granted and that it has caused loss. It has, however, been held that where a local authority is acting in a 'law enforcement' capacity, there is no requirement for such an undertaking to be given. In any action under section 152 of HA 1996 it is likely that an auth-ority will be considered to be acting in this capacity. It is less likely to be considered to be doing so if purely seeking an injunction on the basis of breach of tenancy.

> ### Case report
>
> Coventry City Council had grounds to believe that a spate of crimes on one of its estates, including burglary, harassment, intimidation and fire bombing, were attributable to two brothers. Although the brothers were not tenants, the council obtained an injunction preventing them from entering the area. The order did not contain any undertaking in damages. The injunction was eventually discontinued at the request of the council. The defendants sought an inquiry into damages. It was held that no cross-undertaking in damages was required. Although the judge could have included one at his own discretion, since he had not done so none could be implied.
> *Coventry City Council v Finnie* (1996)

Many of the points in relation to interim injunctions come out in the case of *Southwark London Borough Council v Storrie* (see below). The council was able to obtain a very wide injunction following alleged violent conduct, banning Mr Storrie from his home. The injunction was discharged, however, and an inquiry into damages ordered. The case was partly lost because evidence was not properly put forward at the discharge hearing and was in any event hearsay.

Case report

Southwark London Borough Council obtained an *ex parte* injunction against one of its secure tenants, Mr Storrie. The injunction included a term that the tenant should not return to his home. It also included an undertaking on the issue of damages from the council. The council had acted on reports that the tenant had made a forced entry to a neighbour's flat and made a racially motivated and violent assault with a knife. Criminal charges were eventually dropped, and Mr Storrie applied to discharge the injunction, and also for an inquiry as to damages in respect of the undertaking given by the council. The application to discharge the injunction was allowed, and the inquiry into damages ordered.

The council appealed, against the discharge and the inquiry into damages. The evidence on which the council wished to argue that the injunction ought not to have been discharged – about witness intimidation and that Mr Storrie was a violent man – had not been put before the county court. The Court of Appeal refused to allow consideration of the evidence on appeal because it could have been put to the county court, and in any event it was all hearsay. The council was not in any special position with regard to undertakings in damages simply because it was a public housing authority. Furthermore, it could not be said that, given that the tenant was kept out of his house, any damage he would have suffered would be a 'trivial' injury.

Southwark London Borough Council v Storrie (1996)

Final injunctions

It is quite rare for injunction cases to proceed to final trial. If there has been a breach of an interim injunction then the landlord will almost certainly want to seek possession, and the possession order will overtake the injunction proceedings.

Terms of injunction

Injunctions, whether interim or final, must be set out in sufficiently clear terms for the respondent to know what it is he or she has to do. Where the basis for which the injunction is being sought is breach of the tenancy agreement, it is necessary more than simply to state that the 'tenant should comply with the tenancy conditions'. The specific conduct (e.g. not making an unreasonable noise, not harassing the victim) needs to be spelled out. In certain circumstances of very extreme and dangerous behaviour the court may order that the tenant vacates the premises.

> **Case report**
>
> Residents living in a block of flats accused another tenant of sexual harassment and serious nuisance. Items had been thrown out of the nineteenth-floor flat and witnesses had been threatened. An *ex parte* injunction was granted against the tenant and her family, requiring them to leave the dwelling until the trial. The council undertook to provide them with bed and breakfast accommodation in the interim period. The court made the order on the basis that it was the only way of protecting against the harm being complained of.
> *Hammersmith & Fulham London Borough Council v X* (1990)

See also *Southwark London Borough Council v Storrie* (above) where the Court of Appeal acknowledged that the court had the power to make the initial interim injunction preventing the tenant from returning to his home.

Where an injunction is sought under the Housing Act 1996, section 152(1) sets out the terms of the injunction that may be granted. These are that the person may be prohibited from:

(a) engaging in or threatening to engage in conduct causing or likely to cause a nuisance and annoyance to a person residing in, visiting or otherwise engaging in lawful activity in any dwelling houses held under secure or introductory tenancies from the authority or other accommodation provided by the authority in discharging their duty towards the homeless or in the locality of such premises;

(b) using or threatening to use a dwelling house let under a secure or introductory tenancy from the authority or any other accommodation provided by the authority under the homelessness provisions for immoral or illegal purposes. (In either case the injunction may relate to particular acts or conduct or may be in more general terms.) (Section 152(4)(a) HA 1996);

(c) entering such premises or being found in the locality of such premises. The injunction may specifically relate to particular premises or a particular locality (section 152(4)(b) of HA 1996).

Locality

The term 'locality' is not one that has a clear definition in law. Its extent has already be considered in one case, which although it just predates the coming into force of section 152 was clearly based on the language of the section.

Case report

Manchester City Council sought possession against Ms Lawler, who was a secure tenant of Broadoak Drive in August 1997. At a preliminary hearing of the possession action, Ms Lawler gave six undertakings.

These included that the tenant would not: 'Cause a nuisance, annoyance or disturbance to anyone residing, visiting or otherwise engaging in a lawful activity in the locality of 8, Broadoak Drive.' Other undertakings referred to not using or threatening violence or using abusive or threatening language to those in the locality of the house. The council alleged that Ms Lawler was in breach of the undertakings when she threatened a child with a knife and then threatened the child's mother. The incident with the knife took place on a shopping street on the estate in which Ms Lawler's house was situated. It was just a few minutes' walk from her house.

Following the breach of the undertakings the council sought to have Ms Lawler committed for contempt of court (see further below). The judge refused to do so on the basis that the wording of the undertaking and in particular the words 'in the locality' were too imprecise and unclear. The council appealed. The Court of Appeal referred to section 152 and rejected an argument that any injunction based on it would have to define the locality by roads or by distance. Butler-Sloss L.J. said:

"A defined order relating to specific roads or parts of roads may be either too restrictive or too wide and would not reflect the present wording of the statute and the intention of the legislators. For people living in an area such as a village, a housing estate or so on, there would be in practice little difficulty in knowing what people called the locality. One purpose of the phrase 'in the locality' was to avoid the often difficult, unrewarding and sometimes lengthy discussion about whether to identify one road rather than another, which would meet the general need to keep the tiresome and obstreperous tenant under some control in the area where he/she was likely to the most troublesome. That area may be the part or the whole of a housing estate... In each case it will be a question of fact for the judge whether the place in which the conduct occurred was or was not within the locality..."

On the facts the court held that the incident had taken place within the locality of Ms Lawler's home.
Manchester City Council v Lawler (1998)

Powers of arrest

In the normal course of events, no action can be taken to enforce an injunction until after it has been breached. This is achieved by then returning to court. However, an injunction can be made more draconian by attaching a power of arrest. This can be done only where there is statutory authority for the court to take this action. Section 153 of HA 1996 now provides that a power of arrest may be attached to an injunction which the court intends to grant to deal with an anticipated breach if the applicant is a landlord who is also:

■ a local housing authority
■ a housing action trust
■ a registered social landlord, or
■ a charitable housing trust.

The injunction must be sought against the tenant (or one of joint tenants) under the tenancy agreement (section 153(3) of HA 1996). The tenancy must be either secure, introductory or assured, or of other accommodation provided to the statutorily homeless (section 153(4) of HA 1996). Accordingly, the power of arrest is not available against a long leaseholder who has bought under the right to buy, nor against licensees other than those housed as homeless.

The power can only be attached where the breach or anticipated breach of tenancy consists of the tenant (section 153(5) of HA 1996):

> "(a) engaging in or threatening to engage in conduct causing or likely to cause a nuisance or annoyance to a person residing, visiting or otherwise engaging in a lawful activity in the locality,
>
> (b) using or threatening to use the premises for immoral or illegal purposes, or
>
> (c) allowing any sub-tenant or lodger of his or hers or any other person residing (whether temporarily or otherwise) on the premises or visiting them to act in such a way."

Furthermore the court must decide (1) that the tenant (or any sub-tenant etc) has used or threatened violence against a person residing, visiting or otherwise engaging in lawful activity in the locality, and (2) that there is a significant risk of harm to that or other such person if the power of arrest is not attached to one or more provisions of the injunction immediately (section 153(6) of HA 1996).

A power of arrest may also be attached to an injunction made under section 152 of HA 1996 (see above). In either case, the power may be attached on an *ex parte* application. In making such an order, however, the court must have regard to all the circumstances. In particular, whether the applicant will be 'deterred or prevented' from seeking the order if the power is not exercised immediately (e.g. because witnesses will be intimidated) and whether the respondent (tenant/ perpetrator) is aware of the proceedings but is evading service and any delay will seriously prejudice those living in, visiting or otherwise engaging in lawful activity in the vicinity of the relevant premises (section 154 of HA 1996). If an application is being made for an *ex parte* order to which it is sought to attach a power of arrest, then the affidavits must address these issues.

Effect of a power of arrest

Once a power of arrest has been attached to the injunction a police officer may arrest without warrant any person whom he or she has reasonable cause to suspect is in breach of the injunction or otherwise in contempt of court (section 155(1) of HA 1996). The applicant for the injunction must be informed of the arrest and the person arrested brought before the court (either the High Court or, more normally, the county court) within 24 hours. At the time of writing the full powers of the courts in such cases had not been brought into force, and accordingly the judge must dispose of the matter immediately. Once they have been brought into force, the judge will then have power to remand the person in custody or on bail in accordance with Schedule 15 of HA 1996. Specific provision is also made to remand a person for medical examination and report, and the powers in the Mental Health Act 1983 are applicable to remand for a report on the person's mental condition.

Even where no power of arrest is attached, an application for the issue of a warrant to arrest may be made under section 155(3) of HA 1996 if there has been breach of an injunction. This can only occur where the power of arrest could have been attached but was not.

Effect of breach of injunction

Apart from arrest for breach of an injunction, which is available only in the circumstances set out above, failure to comply with an injunction can be dealt with by committal proceedings. These require that the respondent is personally served with the committal proceedings, including a notice which states how the injunction has been broken (see CCR Order 29, rule 1). Service of this notice will need to be proved at the committal hearing.

Because of the penalties that the courts may impose, before committing someone the judge must be satisfied 'beyond reasonable doubt' that he or she has breached the terms of the injunction. If the breach is proved to this standard, the respondent can be fined or imprisoned for up to two years (see RSC Order 52 in the High Court, section 4 of the Contempt of Court Act 1981, and the County Courts (Penalties for Contempt) Act 1983 in the county court). The imprisonment may be suspended, which is the most likely outcome of a first single breach. Where the breach of injunction is by someone aged between 18 and 21 they must be committed to a young offenders institution rather than a prison (section 9 of the Criminal Justice Act 1982 (as amended)). Those under 18 cannot be committed to prison (see p. 83 below).

> **Case report**
>
> **The London Borough of Southwark obtained an injunction against a tenant, Mr Kennedy, who was abusing his elderly Scottish neighbours. When he breached the injunction by hammering on the ceiling of his flat, blocking entrances with his three dogs and launching an 'anti-Scottish tirade' against the neighbours, he was imprisoned for 28 days.**
> *Southwark London Borough Council v Kennedy* (1996)

See also *Leicester City Council v March and others* (below p. 79) for an example of imprisonment for contempt for breach of an injunction by non-tenants.

Anti-social behaviour orders

Authorities may also be able to seek an anti-social behaviour order against a tenant in appropriate circumstances. The basis for making orders and their scope will be the same whether the defendant is a tenant or a non-tenant. They are more likely to be used against non-tenants, particularly children, and are considered in detail at pp. 85-87 below.

Possession

The ultimate sanction against the tenant is to obtain possession of the property. For social landlords the majority of tenants are either secure or assured; consequently possession must therefore be sought in accordance with either the HA 1985 or the HA 1988. The position of introductory tenants is considered in Chapter 3 above.

In order to obtain possession against a secure or assured tenant the landlord must be able to show that a ground for possession is available, and then obtain a court order based on that ground (see further A. Dymond, *Security of*

Tenure (Arden's Housing Library) 1995). There are two main grounds that are relevant in cases of anti-social behaviour: breach of tenancy (Ground 1 of HA 1985 and Ground 12 of HA 1988) and nuisance or criminal conduct (Ground 2 of HA 1985 and Ground 14 of HA 1988). Under both Acts the grounds fall within those which are discretionary, so that as well as proving that the conduct took place it is necessary to convince the court that it is reasonable to make an order for possession.

Breach of tenancy

Grounds 1 and 12 simply state that the possession may be granted for breach of a term of the tenancy. In many cases the conduct complained of will also fall within Grounds 2 and 14 (see below). A well-drawn tenancy agreement may, however, go beyond this. It is also helpful to use breach of tenancy agreement, where the agreement sets out specific conduct which is unacceptable. The fact that the tenancy specifically sets out what is unacceptable behaviour, and that the tenant was therefore aware of this from the start of the tenancy may assist in persuading a judge that it is reasonable to grant possession.

Nuisance and criminal conduct

Grounds 2 and 14 were significantly altered by the Housing Act 1996. They now read as follows:

> "The tenant or a person residing in or visiting the dwelling-house –
> (a) has been guilty of conduct causing or likely to cause a nuisance or annoyance to a person residing, visiting or otherwise engaging in a lawful activity in the locality, or
> (b) has been convicted of –
>   (i) using the dwelling-house or allowing it to be used for immoral or illegal purposes, or
>   (ii) an arrestable offence committed in, or in the locality of the dwelling-house."

Conduct causing or likely to cause nuisance or annoyance

Nuisance under Grounds 2 and 14 does not require nuisance in a technical sense, but in a natural sense and, in any event, annoyance is a term with a wider meaning. It must be such as would annoy an ordinary occupier, not an ultra-sensitive one (*Tod-Heatly v Benham* (1888)).

As previously worded, Grounds 2 and 14 did not refer to conduct 'likely to cause' a nuisance. The extension of the Grounds is intended to make it easier to obtain possession without the actual victim having to give evidence, since it is now not necessary to prove that the behaviour did in fact cause a nuisance to a particular person. Thus the evidence could come from a third party, such as an environmental health officer or police officer. The third party will, however, have to witness the conduct complained of; it is not sufficient for a housing officer to simply recount the complaints that have been made to him or her, since that is hearsay evidence (although see p. 128 below on the use of hearsay evidence). In cases of noise nuisance it should be sufficient to use measurements of the noise levels where environmental health officers have monitored these.

'Persons residing, visiting or otherwise engaging in a lawful activity...'

Prior to amendment the Ground simply referred to nuisance and annoyance caused to neighbours. As it is now, a much wider range of victims is encompassed. Visitors and those otherwise engaged in lawful activity include members of the landlord's staff, members of the emergency services (it has not been uncommon for fire engines to come under attack when entering estates) and workmen carrying out repair work. The term 'in the locality' is not one that has a clear definition in law, and it remains to be seen how the courts will apply it (see *Manchester City Council v Lawler*, above). It may be that a school comes within the locality of the tenant's home, as may local shops. Even under the unamended

Ground, 'neighbour' was given a wide definition by the Court of Appeal in *Northampton Borough Council v Lovatt* (1997) so as to encompass all persons sufficiently close to the source of conduct complained of to be adversely affected by it.

Illegal and immoral use

This part of the ground is unchanged from the old one, and it has been held that the conviction for an immoral or illegal purpose must be directly linked to the property.

Case report

The tenant was convicted for the possession of cannabis. There had been evidence at the criminal trial that some of the drug had been found at her flat. The landlord sought possession on the basis of a conviction for using the premises for an immoral or illegal purpose. The judge refused to grant possession on the basis that the landlord had not established illegal *use* of the premises. Furthermore he decided that it was not, in any event, reasonable to make an order for possession.

The landlord's appeal was dismissed. While it was not necessary for the conviction relied on to relate specifically to the premises of which possession was sought, the landlord was required to adduce satisfactory evidence to prove illegal use of the premises. This had not been done. Simply finding the tenant on the premises in possession of drugs did not amount to using the premises in connection with the offence. It would, however, have been sufficient if the premises were being used to store or hide the drugs, if this evidence had been available.

Abrahams v Wilson (1971)

Arrestable offence

Under section 24 of the Police and Criminal Evidence Act 1984 an 'arrestable offence' means any offence:

1. which bears a fixed penalty (e.g. murder);
2. from which a first offender aged 21 or over could be sent to prison for five or more years (this includes all serious offences, including robbery, assault causing actual bodily harm and burglary);
3. specifically identified as such.

There is a long list of identified offences. It includes taking a vehicle without authority (section 12(1) of the Theft Act 1968); a number of offences relating to carrying offensive weapons and knives; and publishing material intended or likely to stir up racial hatred (section 19 of the Public Order Act 1986). Harassment contrary to section 1 of the Protection from Harassment Act 1997 and the new offence of racially aggravated harassment in the Crime and Disorder Act 1998 are both arrestable offences.

Procedure for obtaining possession

Before the case can be brought to court various steps should be complied with, which we now consider in turn.

Warning letters

There is no statutory requirement that warning letters be sent to the tenant. However, in most cases it is good practice to do so. If it can be shown that the tenant received warning letters and still persisted with the conduct then it makes it more likely that the judge will find it reasonable to grant possession (see below). Where there has been an increasing problem on a particular estate many landlords send 'round robin' letters reminding tenants of their responsibilities. It is always useful to ensure that copies of these are kept on file. Again they will make it harder for tenants to say when they are accused of particular behaviour that they were unaware that they were causing a problem or were in breach of their tenancy.

Notice of seeking possession

Before a court can order possession under the Housing Act 1985 or 1988 the landlord must first serve a notice of seeking possession (see A. Dymond, *Security of Tenure* (Arden's Housing Library) 1995, Ch. 5). The notice must set out not just the ground on which possession is being sought but also details of the ground so that the tenant can know what it is that he or she must do to put matters right (*Torridge District Council v Jones* (1985)). Although that case concerned the setting out of rent arrears, care should be taken in drafting the notice where nuisance is being alleged. Where Ground 1 or 12 is being relied on, the notice should set out the term which it is alleged is being breached. All allegations of nuisance and annoyance should be set out clearly, preferably with dates and specific details.

> *Case report*
>
> **Slough Borough Council sought possession under Grounds 1 and 2 of HA 1985 Act on the basis of noise nuisance. The notice failed to state what term of the tenancy had been breached. In relation to Ground 2 it simply stated that 'numerous complaints have been received over a period of time that annoyance and nuisance has been caused to neighbours by noise and disruptive behaviour...'. The notice was held to be inadequate because the allegations of nuisance and annoyance were insufficiently particularised.**
> **Slough Borough Council v Robbins (1997)**

Generally the notice must give a particular period which must expire before the landlord may proceed to court. The procedure has, however, been modified where possession is sought under Grounds 2 or 14. In either case, possession proceedings may be commenced immediately on service of the notice of seeking possession (section 83(3) of HA 1985; section 8(4) of HA 1988). In the case of a secure tenancy the notice must specify a date on which the tenant is asked to give up possession. The new notice procedure is intended to speed up the possession process so that proceedings may be issued on the same day that the notice of seeking possession is served on the tenant.

Reasonable to continue to occupy

Under all the relevant grounds the court has discretion over whether to grant possession, and must decide, once the behaviour has been proved, if it is reasonable for the tenant to continue occupation of the premises. The court can take anything relevant into account in reaching such a decision, but a number of factors should be addressed in particular, and a discussion of these follows.

Effect on victims

One important factor which courts should not underestimate is the effect that the behaviour has had on the victims. The Court of Appeal has stated on a number of occasions that tenants should not have to put up with harassment (see e.g. *Kensington & Chelsea Royal Borough Council v Simmonds* (1996) (below p. 88), *Darlington Borough Council v Sterling* (1996) (below p. 70) and *West Kent Housing Association v Davies* (1998) (below p. 73).

> *Case report*
>
> **Mr Bistram was the secure tenant of Woking District Council. His neighbours complained of the threats and foul language that he used towards them. At the trial the judge found that the conduct was still continuing 'as far as that is relevant', but decided that bad language was 'no doubt very much a common experience in certain areas' and refused to order possession. The council appealed successfully. The fact that the nuisance was continuing was highly relevant to the proceedings. The judge's view about**

> local behaviour was unsupported by any evidence and
> should not have been taken into account. The coun-
> cil's obligations to other tenants were plainly material
> and had not been taken into account sufficiently.
> *Woking Borough Council v Bistram* (1993)

Effect on tenant

To be balanced in the equation is the effect the order will
have on the tenant and other members of his or her family.
However, even where the tenant has children this does not
mean that it is unreasonable to order possession unless the
court is satisfied that alternative accommodation will be provided. The court should not try and second-guess the decisions of homeless persons units: it is sufficient for the court
to know that the applicant will be entitled to make an application as homeless, and that it will be dealt with properly.

Case report

Mrs Sterling was a secure tenant of Darlington
Borough Council. She lived in a house with her two
children, a son aged 13 and a daughter aged 12. The
housing authority sought possession under Ground 2
of the Housing Act 1985, because of the son's activities. He had lit fires, thrown stones, made threats
with knives and carried out assaults. At the trial the
district judge found that the behaviour was proved.
In deciding whether it was reasonable to grant possession he took into account that the tenant had
done her best to control her son and would face difficulties in finding other accommodation. He decided nonetheless to grant possession, since the
neighbours should not have to endure the son's behaviour. In passing, the district judge expressed the
view that the behaviour was not the tenant's fault and
that she should not be found intentionally homeless.

The tenant appealed to the circuit judge who
overturned the finding of possession. He held that
although Ground 2 did not require that suitable

alternative accommodation be made available, given that the district judge had found that the authority should re-house the tenant it was not reasonable to make an order for possession unless suitable alternative accommodation was available. In the absence of any evidence that such accommodation was available the circuit judge decided it was not reasonable to grant possession.

On appeal to the Court of Appeal, the original order for possession was restored. The Court emphasised that the question of suitable alternative accommodation was not relevant to deciding whether to grant possession under Ground 2. It was relevant to consider the effect on the tenant and others, if the order is made. It was also relevant, however, to consider the effect on the neighbours of *not* making the order for possession. The court could not refuse an order for possession unless the authority provided suitable alternative accommodation.
Darlington Borough Council v Sterling (1996)

Breach of injunction

Where an injunction has been obtained and is then breached, this is strong evidence that nothing short of outright possession is the appropriate order.

Time delay

The period of time that has elapsed since the tenant has been a nuisance is relevant. Generally the longer the gap, the less likely it is that it will be reasonable to make an order for possession.

Case report

Mr Hargreaves was the secure tenant of a flat owned by Wandsworth London Borough Council. It was a term of the tenancy that the tenant would 'ensure that he, his household and visitors comply with the tenancy conditions and use the premises and the communal areas in a manner which does not cause any discomfort, inconvenience, nuisance, annoyance to or damage to the personal property of other people...'

On the evening of 25 March 1991, Mr Hargreaves was present in the flat with two other people. He had been drinking, but claimed that he knew what he was doing. His companions had brought a canister of petrol and were making fire bombs. Mr Hargreaves stated that he had not realised that this was what they were doing. One of the others threw the bombs out of a window in the flat onto a truck outside; his sleeve caught fire and the petrol canister spilt and ignited when Mr Hargreaves lit a cigarette. As a result the flat was seriously damaged.

The housing authority repaired the flat. Mr Hargreaves was allowed to return into occupation in June 1992, the authority having been advised that it had no option but to do so. The authority commenced possession on the basis of breach of tenancy. The matter came to court in February 1993 and the judge found that it was not reasonable to make an order for possession, since there had been no further complaints in respect of Mr Hargreaves' conduct. The Court of Appeal upheld this decision, stating that when deciding whether to make a possession order the court should look at the relevant circumstances up to the date when the hearing takes place, and whether there had been further misconduct during that period was plainly relevant.

Wandsworth London Borough Council v Hargreaves (1994)

In some instances, however, the reason that the matter has not been brought to court quickly is because of delays by the tenant. When this is the case it will be less relevant that a long period of time has elapsed since the conduct complained of. In *Bristol City Council v Mousah* (see p. 95, below) by the time the matter came to court there had been no breaches of the tenancy for over a year. The Court of Appeal did not consider this significant, partly because of the seriousness of the conduct (permitting drug dealing from the premises) and also because the lapse of time was largely due to the tenant's failure to comply with court orders to deliver his defence.

Where the conduct has continued until the time of the trial this is a very strong indicator that possession should be granted.

Suspended or outright possession?

Once the court has decided that it is reasonable to make an order for possession, the possession order can then be suspended or can be implemented outright. It is not unusual in nuisance cases for the court to make a suspended order, conditional on cessation of the conduct. In the *Bistram* case, above, the Court of Appeal made a suspended order, emphasising that if there was the slightest repetition of the conduct outright possession should be obtained. In *Kensington & Chelsea Royal Borough Council v Simmonds* (see p. 88, below) the judge suspended the order on condition that there were no further incidents of nuisance or annoyance or racial abuse to a neighbouring family. The order was made effective for just over a year. The Court of Appeal upheld the order, despite arguments from the tenant that it was insufficiently clear what would amount to a breach. The Court found that it was clear enough for the tenant's son to understand what was required of him. In *West Kent Housing Association Ltd v Davies* (1998), where the tenant's son had been responsible for racial abuse, and the tenants had worked on motor vehicles late into the night and been abusive to neighbours, the Court of Appeal overturned the refusal of the judge to order possession, and replaced it with a possession order suspended for two years.

In serious cases, such as drug dealing or violence, it is not appropriate to make a suspended order, and outright possession should be granted: see *Bristol City Council v Mousah*, p. 95 below.

5.
Nuisance Behaviour by Particular Groups

Terms of tenancy / Non-tenant adults / Children /
Owner-occupiers / Vulnerable perpetrators

The steps that can be taken to deal with perpetrators who are
not tenants of the landlord are examined in this chapter.
Those responsible for the conduct complained of may
be other members of the tenant's household or visitors to
the household, whether children or adults. A perpetrator
might also be an owner-occupier who has, for example,
bought under the right to buy. Finally we consider the
particular difficulties which may arise when the perpetrator
is a vulnerable adult.

Terms of tenancy

In order to take action against the tenant because of conduct
by other people who are members of, or visitors to, the tenant's
household it is important that the tenancy agreement has
been framed broadly enough. Whether the tenant is in breach
of the terms of the tenancy depends on the specific wording.
In relation to family members and other lodgers and visitors
it is not unusual that the prohibition is phrased in terms of
the tenant not 'allowing' or 'permitting' the behaviour.

In *Kensington & Chelsea Royal Borough Council v Simmonds*
(1996) (see p. 88, below) the relevant clauses of the authority's

tenancy agreement stated that the tenant should not 'allow any discomfort, inconvenience or any annoyance to his neighbours whether by himself or members of his household including lodgers visitors or animals'. Furthermore, the tenant should not 'allow members of his household or invited visitors to commit any act which may interfere with the peace and comfort or cause offence to any other tenant . . . by reason of his race, colour, ethnic origin or nationality'. One of the questions that the court had to consider was whether the tenant had 'allowed' her 13-year-old son to commit the racial abuse complained of. The conduct had continued over a period of months, and although the judge had accepted that the tenant found it very difficult to control her son, it was held that she had 'allowed' the conduct. If there had been only one single unheralded incident then it could not have been said that the tenant allowed it, but that was not the case here.

A similar approach was taken in *West Kent Housing Association Ltd v Davies* (1998) where the tenant's son had again been involved in racial abuse. Even if there is no approval or encouragement of the behaviour the tenant can be responsible for failing to prevent the abuse where the tenancy agreement makes the tenant responsible for 'permitting' or 'allowing' the behaviour.

Non-tenant adults

Where the perpetrator of anti-social behaviour is not the tenant of the landlord the remedies for breach of tenancy, leading to either an injunction or possession, are not available directly. Thus it is necessary to consider, (1) on what other bases an injunction may be obtained against such an adult; (2) whether an injunction may also be obtainable against the tenant for 'permitting the behaviour'; and (3) whether possession may be obtained against the tenant again for permitting the behaviour. It may also be possible to obtain an anti-social behaviour order against such a person. These are considered in detail at p. 85 below.

Injunctions

To obtain an injunction a plaintiff must have a legal cause of action (see pp. 49-51 above). Where the perpetrator is not the tenant it is not possible to take action on the basis of breach of contract, as there is no contractual relationship between the landlord and the perpetrator. It is therefore necessary to consider other bases for the action. Where the landlord is a local authority the most obvious is under the section 152 of HA 1996. This is discussed in detail in Chapter 4 and operates in exactly the same way whether the person against whom the injunction is sought is a tenant or not. It may be easier, however, to obtain injunctions banning non-tenants from a particular area, since this is much less of an interference with their property rights.

As discussed in Chapter 4, section 152 is applicable only in cases of actual or threatened violence. Thus it is not applicable to all situations where landlords wish to take action. Furthermore it is not available to non-local authority social landlords. It is necessary therefore to consider on what other bases an injunction may be sought.

Nuisance

The 'essence of nuisance is a condition or activity which unduly interferes with the use or enjoyment of land' (*Clerk and Lindsell on Torts*, quoted with approval in *Khorasandjian v Bush* (1993)). In order for a landlord (as opposed to the direct victim such as a neighbour) to act on the basis of behaviour amounting to a nuisance the landlord must be able to show that his or her use of enjoyment of the land has been interfered with. On this basis it was decided in a number of older cases that a landlord who had let his or her property could not take action where the nuisance was one that merely annoyed the lessee, such as noise and smell, since it might stop at any point before the end of the lease. This was true even where the property was let on a weekly tenancy (see e.g. *Jones v Chappell* (1875)).

A more 'generous' view was taken by contrast in *Hampstead and Suburban Properties v Diomedous* (1969). The case was primarily about the enforcement of the terms of a lease but the argument was made that the nuisance caused by loud music in a restaurant only affected the neighbouring tenants and did not affect the landlord. The judge rejected the contention as 'absurd' and he pointed to the likely effects on the landlord of diminution in value of the property, of complaints from the tenants and difficulty in re-letting.

So it may well be possible in cases of severe nuisance to argue that the landlord has the basis of a cause of action in nuisance.

Trespass

Where adults who are not tenants are behaving in an anti-social manner it may well be the case that they are doing it in common parts of the landlord's property and on other land (e.g. vacant properties) belonging to the landlord. If they have no lawful reason to be on that land, they are trespassing. Trespass is a tort and an injunction can be sought to prevent it occurring.

Local Government Act 1972

Local authorities are given powers under section 222 of the 1972 Act to take legal proceedings where the authority considers it is expedient to do so 'for the promotion or protection of the interests of the inhabitants of their area.' In order to act under this section it is not necessary to show that the local authority has had its own legal rights infringed.

A number of authorities have used section 222 to seek injunctions against non-tenant perpetrators. An injunction cannot be granted under this section simply because the authority does not approve of the behaviour. In this sense it does not directly get round the 'cause of action' problem. It is still necessary to show some legal basis for the claim for injunction.

As already stated, this does not have to be a direct infringement of the authority's legal rights. Most commonly injunctions have been granted under this section to prevent breaches of the criminal law, e.g. drug dealing, burglary, intimidation. It would be possible to seek an injunction on the basis of section 222 to prevent the alleged perpetrator from carrying on the conduct or, more likely, from entering the particular area where the conduct is being perpetrated. Action under section 222 may also be justified where a nuisance is being committed which affects a large number of inhabitants in the area.

Acting on victim's behalf

One other way in which legal action may be taken is for the landlord to act on the victim's behalf, conducting the litigation in the victim's name but in essence paying for and arranging it all. It may be possible to launch a combined action, with the landlord also seeking redress in its own right, as well as underwriting the victim's action. Two issues must be addressed if such action is going to be taken. First, does the landlord have the power to take the action? Secondly, has a proper agreement been reached between the victim and the landlord?

Powers

Local authorities are not free agents and any action that they take must have some explicit or implicit statutory legal authority. There is nothing that expressly authorises them to initiate legal proceedings on behalf of other individuals (as opposed to actions for the good of the inhabitants of their area as a whole, see above.). However, under section 111 of LGA 1972 a local authority may 'do anything . . . which is calculated to facilitate, or is conducive or incidental to the discharge of their functions.' Authorities have a general power to manage their housing properties under section 21 of HA 1985. It may well be arguable that assisting an individual in a particular case is 'calculated to facilitate' this function.

Registered social landlords are less constrained about what action they can enter into, although before making a commitment to any action on behalf of tenants regard must be had to the constitution of the organisation and advice from the Housing Corporation.

Agreement with the victim
Where action is being taken on behalf of an individual victim the arrangements must be clearly understood from the outset, and preferably recorded in writing. The victim must understand that he or she is a named party in the proceedings and in consequence has responsibilities to support the litigation. Ultimately both the victim and the landlord must be able to withdraw from the proceedings, and the arrangements must cover what action is to be taken in those circumstances.

An agreement must also cover the position if the litigation fails in the end. This may require payment not only of the victim's costs but also those of the defendant. Landlords must be willing to take on this responsibility if they are genuinely to cover the victim's liability.

Success of such actions

In a number of fairly high-profile cases local authorities have successfully taken action against non-tenant adults. A useful example of what can be achieved is taken from action of Leicester City Council on the Eyres Monsell Estate.

Case report

A gang of youths was causing serious damage and intimidating residents on the Eyres Monsell Estate in Leicester. One particular family ('the Todds') was a target of their attacks, and the Todds' home was invaded. The authority sought injunctions against four youths that forbade them to enter a specific area of the estate and from assaulting the Todds. The judge made the orders sought on 24 June 1996, although it was time limited. The youths breached the injunction on several occasions and the matter came back for committal. The judge found that the youths had shown 'a flagrant disregard' for the injunction. He sentenced the three who were aged under 21 to a total of nine months in a young offenders institution, and the fourth to a similar term in prison. On release from prison early in 1997, two of the youths, brothers John and James March, were again involved in incidents on the estate, including one where Mrs Todd was abused by a gang. The authority had already decided to start possession proceedings against the youths' mother (see below), and as part of those proceedings permanent injunctions were sought against the March brothers preventing them from assaulting the Todds and from entering the estate. The injunctions were granted by the judge 'until further order' so that if they wished to enter the area they had to apply for leave from the court to do so.

Leicester City Council v March and others; Leicester City Council v Hart and others (unreported, transcripts kindly supplied by Feizal Hajat, Leicester City Council).

Injunctions against tenant

Where the tenancy agreement makes the tenant responsible for the actions of those residing in or visiting the property it may be possible to seek an injunction against the tenant. The terms of any injunction must be considered very carefully to ensure that they are clear enough to convince a court that they are enforceable. Some courts are willing to grant injunctions on the basis that 'the defendant is forbidden from permitting their family or visitors from causing a nuisance or annoyance to neighbours'. Nonetheless it is more usually the case that the more vague the terms of the injunction the less likely it will be that the tenant can successfully be committed for breach. It may also be possible, in some circumstances, to seek an injunction requiring the tenant not to admit the perpetrator to the property.

Possession

Where adult members of the household, lodgers or visitors are themselves responsible for anti-social behaviour, possession may be sought against the tenant. This may be done on the basis either of breach of the tenancy conditions (Grounds 1 and 12) or breach of the specific grounds relating to anti-social behaviour (Grounds 2 and 14) (see further Chapter 4, above). It should be noted that where a breach of grounds 2 or 14 is alleged against a person residing in or visiting the dwelling-house (see p. 64, above) there is no requirement that the tenants have any knowledge of the behaviour (see *West Kent Housing Association Ltd v Davies* (1998)), although this may be a relevant factor as to whether it is reasonable to grant possession. Whether there is a breach of the tenancy is discussed above at p. 74.

Reasonableness of granting possession

Once it has been shown that all the necessary elements of the ground for possession have been made out, the court has to consider whether it is reasonable to make an order for possession. The court may be more willing to find that it is not reasonable to grant possession if the tenant can show that he or she took steps to stop the behaviour. However, as with children (p. 87, below), there is no reason to refuse possession simply because matters were beyond the tenant's control.

Case reports

The tenant Ms Blake, had two adult sons who played loud music during the late evening and early hours. Her landlord, Leicester District Council, sought possession. The sons, aged 19 and 23, had had their equipment seized by environmental health officers on two occasions, but had bought another sound system for a party just a week before the case was due to be heard. The tenant claimed that she was unable to control her sons, and the judge found that she was unwilling to take the final step of actually evicting them. The authority had made offers of flats to the two sons, to which neither of them had responded. The judge made an order for possession, making it clear that the tenant was responsible for the behaviour of her sons while they lived in her home. The judge refused to suspend the order for possession because of the numerous times on which, despite warnings, the tenant had failed to take any action. She should, but was not willing to, evict her sons and accordingly an outright order was appropriate. *Leicester District City Council v Blake* (1997) (additional information from transcript).

*

In *Leicester City Council v Hart* in addition to seeking permanent injunctions against John and James March, the authority also sought possession against their mother, Ms Hart. The judge found that she took no active steps to control them, although she knew about their behaviour. Furthermore it was clear that any steps she might take would be ineffectual. Although the two sons were not living at the house permanently the judge found that they would be likely to resume their behaviour if the mother stayed in the home, using the mother's home as a base. An outright order for possession was required in order to protect the other residents on the estate from their behaviour. *Leicester City Council v Hart* (1997)

It may be appropriate to refuse possession where the tenant has taken steps to stop the perpetrator coming to the property, or the perpetrator has otherwise been removed from the scene (e.g. because he or she has been imprisoned). In serious cases this should not prevent an order for possession.

> **Case report**
>
> **Ms Wilson was the tenant of Blyth Valley District Council. She lived in the property with her two children and her boyfriend. The boyfriend was convicted of supplying heroin from the property and jailed for four years. The council sought to evict Ms Wilson. The court made an order for outright possession, having found that Ms Wilson was well aware of her boyfriend's activities.**
> *Blyth Valley District Council v Wilson* **(1996)**

Children

Children (i.e. those under 18) are responsible for much of the anti-social behaviour of which complaint is made. This gives rise to many legal problems as the law does not treat children in the same way as adults. This is particularly true in relation to injunctions.

Injunctions

Injunctions may be sought against either the child or his or her parents, although in both cases there are considerable problems that may be encountered to which we now turn.

Against child perpetrators

In general it is not possible to obtain injunctions against children. The reasoning behind this is that because injunctions could not be enforced there is no point in granting them in the first place (see *Wookey v Wookey, Re S (a minor)* (1991)). As set out above (p. 62) the way in which injunctions are enforced is either by imprisonment or by fine. The civil courts have no power to imprison children (powers to imprison children are carefully controlled by statute). Furthermore most children do not have any adequate income from which a fine can be paid. But this is not always true: some 16 and 17- year-olds may be in employment or on training schemes. It should not always be assumed therefore that no injunctive action could be taken. Careful enquiry should be made to establish the age of alleged perpetrators and whether they have a potential income against which a fine could be levied. If they do, then injunctive action on the same basis as is set out above against non-tenant adults may be contemplated.

The difficulties of the situation are illustrated by the problems encountered by Croydon London Borough Council.

Case report

Croydon London Borough Council was faced with an escalating problem of racism on the Monk's Hill Estate. The behaviour included criminal damage, threats of violence and abuse. The authority sought injunctions against five named youths and their parents. The youths were aged between 12 and 18. The injunctions were initially granted and prevented the youths from assaulting, molesting, abusing or threatening a named family on the estate (*Inside Housing*, 17 May 1996). The injunctions were successful in preventing the behaviour and reducing the harassment that was happening on the estate.

One of the families, however, applied to have the injunction discharged against both the parents and their 12-year-old son. The court discharged the injunction against the 12-year-old on the basis that, in the light of *Wookey v Wookey*, it should not have been made in the first place. The injunction against the parents was discharged on the basis that their

> involvement had been 'grossly overstated' in the
> council's affidavit.
> *Croydon London Borough Council v M and others* (1996)

Injunctions against the parents

Even where the parents are not directly involved in the anti-social behaviour, it may be possible to obtain an injunction against them for breach of the tenancy agreement, if it includes a term that they will ensure that their children will not be a nuisance and annoyance to neighbours. However, while there may be a failure by tenants to comply with this condition, seeking an injunction on the basis of breach of it presents particular difficulties. The parent cannot be required simply to exclude the child from the home, as may happen with adult perpetrators (see p. 80 above), since they have an on-going legal responsibility for the child.

It may be possible to obtain an injunction requiring the tenant parent to comply with the tenancy terms not to permit the child to carry out the nuisance. The problem with this is the exact wording that will be necessary. The tenant parent may well say that he or she has done all he or she can to control the child. The court would not grant an injunction requiring the parent to do any more than take reasonable and defined steps to control the child. If there is still anti-social behaviour by the child this would not be a breach of the injunction by the parent. For this reason there may be little future in seeking injunctions in these circumstances and it would be better to move directly to seeking possession.

Anti-social behaviour orders

The problems of gaining injunctions against non-tenants and children in particular appear to be one of the main justifications for the government introducing the anti-social behaviour order in the Crime and Disorder Act 1998. The orders are available against anyone aged 10 or over (section 1(1) of CDA 1998). At the time of writing the provisions had not yet been brought into force. It is expected that extensive guidance will be given when they are brought into force, which seems likely to be April 1999.

Conditions for making an order

The court may make an order only if three conditions are satisfied (section 1(1)):

■ the person has acted in an anti-social manner, defined as 'in a manner that caused or was likely to cause alarm or distress'

■ the alarm or distress must be caused to one or more persons who are not members of the same household as the person against whom the order is made

■ the order is necessary to protect persons in the authority's area from further anti-social acts or conduct.

It is to be noted that there is no specific spatial context to the behaviour. It can take place anywhere in the local authority's area. Those who are affected by it need not be in any sense neighbours, nor indeed is there any link with the local authority's tenants. The order may be sought against anyone in the area.

Applying for an order

The order is to be made by a magistrates court, and an anti-social behaviour order may be applied for either by the police or by the local authority (section 1(1)). Whichever one seeks to make the application must first consult with the other (section 1(2)). The application must be made to the magistrates' court by complaint (section 1(3)). In deciding whether a defendant has acted in an anti-social manner, the court must disregard behaviour that is shown to be reasonable in the circumstances (section 1(5)). The reference to the word 'complaint' indicates that this first stage is intended to be treated as a civil matter in the magistrates court (see section 51 of Magistrates Courts Act 1980). As such the court will have the power to proceed in the defendant's absence (section 55 of MCA 1980), and proof will be to a civil standard, i.e. on the balance of probabilities.

Terms of the order

If the necessary conditions are proved then the court may make an anti-social behaviour order which prohibits the defendant from doing anything which the court considers necessary 'for the purpose of protecting persons in the . . . area from further anti-social acts by the defendant'. This gives an extremely wide discretion to the court, but could include banning defendants from a particular area of the authority for some or all of the time, e.g. between 6 p.m. and midnight. The order will last for a minimum period of two years, unless varied or discharged (section 1(7) and (8)). It cannot be discharged in less than two years without the consent of both parties (section 1(9)).

Effect of breach

Breach of an anti-social behaviour order without reasonable excuse will be a criminal offence, which may be tried in either the magistrates' or crown court (section 1(10) of CDA 1998). Magistrates will have power to imprison those in breach for up to six months or fine up to the statutory maximum (section 1(10)(a)). The crown court will be able to imprison for up to five years and/or fine (section 1(10)(b)). In the case of those aged 21 and under, these powers will be subject to the specifically limited powers, some of which are affected by provisions in the Crime and Disorder Act itself. The power for the courts conditionally to discharge those convicted is explicitly excluded by section 1(11).

Possession

Where anti-social behaviour is being carried out by children possession may be sought against the parents. This may be done either on the basis of breach of the tenancy conditions (Grounds 1 and 12) or breach of the specific grounds relating to anti-social behaviour (Grounds 2 and 14). Whether there is a breach of the tenancy is discussed above at p. 74.

Reasonableness of granting possession

There is no reason simply because the perpetrators are children to refuse possession against the parents. In *Darlington Borough Council v Sterling* (p. 70, above) the court overturned a refusal to grant possession against a tenant whose 13-year-old son had been guilty of anti-social behaviour. The courts must always consider the effect on the victims if possession is refused.

Case report

The tenant, Ms Simmonds, was the secure tenant of a flat owned by Kensington & Chelsea Royal Borough Council. She lived there with her 13-year-old-son. The son and his friends had caused considerable inconvenience and annoyance to a neighbouring Pakistani family, the Ahmeds, between 5 June and 1 October 1994. There had been at least two occasions when the son had used racist language. The judge found that it was reasonable to make an order for possession under both Grounds 1 and 2 of HA 1985. The judge decided, however, to suspend the order on condition that there were no further incidents of annoyance or racial abuse directed against the Ahmeds. The order was expressed to be effective for one year and 14 days. The tenant appealed.

The Court of Appeal upheld the order. The tenant was found to have 'allowed' the behaviour (see above p. 74), and accordingly there had been a breach of the tenancy conditions. The extent of

> blame on the tenant's part was a relevant consider-
> ation in deciding whether to grant possession.
> Nonetheless possession could be granted where a
> tenant had tried and failed to control her child. The
> court had to weigh up not only the interests of the
> tenant and her family but also those of the neigh-
> bours, who should not be deprived of relief simply
> because the tenant was incapable of controlling her son.
> *Kensington & Chelsea Royal Borough Council v
> Simmonds* (1996)

Social Services' powers

Where children are beyond the control of their parents, rather
than seeking to evict the parents, it may be appropriate to
seek assistance from social services. See J. Henderson, *Children
and Housing* (Arden's Housing Library) forthcoming.

Owner-occupiers

Thus far the book has addressed the issue of anti-social
behaviour on the basis that the perpetrator is either a tenant
of a social landlord or in some way connected to a tenant.
Yet this is not always the case. Anti-social behaviour is not
confined by tenure (although much of the Housing Act 1996
provisions seem to make this assumption), and social landlords may well encounter anti-social behaviour being perpetrated by owner-occupiers and their families. Anti-social
behaviour orders (see p. 74, above) will be available against
owner-occupiers and their families.

Exercise of right to buy

One particular problem that has arisen relates to tenants who
are seeking to exercise their right to buy under the Housing
Act 1985, while at the same time the landlord is seeking to

evict them for anti-social behaviour. Once a possession order has been granted the tenants loses his or her right to buy (section 121 of HA 1985; see further J. Henderson, *Rights to Buy and Acquire* (Arden's Housing Library), 1997). Where, however, the tenant completes all the necessary stages of the right to buy – so that the price and terms are agreed prior to any possession order being obtained – the tenant has the right to enforce the sale. Where, however, possession proceedings are also pending, e.g. for nuisance allegations, the court may decide in which order to hear the cases. (*Bristol City Council v Lovell* (1997)). This issue is discussed in more detail in J. Henderson, *Rights to Buy and Acquire*: pp. 104-105.

Covenants

Where a social landlord sells the property, be it under the right to buy, the right to acquire or voluntarily, it may chose to put covenants in the sale relating to anti-social behaviour. Where land is being sold as freehold it is possible to insert covenants expressed to be for the benefit of the land retained by the landlord which will be binding on the initial purchaser and subsequent purchasers. Such covenants must be expressed in a negative form (i.e. 'not to be a nuisance and annoyance to occupiers of the adjoining land retained by the vendor'). Local authorities also have additional powers to enforce such covenants against subsequent owners under section 33 of the Local Government (Miscellaneous Provisions) Act 1982. An injunction is usually required to enforce compliance with such freehold covenants.

Landlords should always seek to include appropriate terms where properties are sold on long leases. There is no reason why these should not be in the same form as those used for short-term tenants. Such terms can then be enforced through injunction, and ultimately, in the case of severe breaches, by seeking forfeiture of the long lease. Although this is a serious step, which the court would require some convincing to take, there is no reason why in appropriate cases (e.g. serious criminal activity such as drug dealing) the court should not grant forfeiture of the lease for the breach of such a term. (On forfeiture, see D. Kilcoyne, *Leaseholder Management* (Arden's Housing Library) 1997: Ch. 9.) Landlords should not overlook this as a possible course of action.

The power of arrest granted by section 153 of HA 1996 (see above p. 60) is not available where an injunction is being sought for breach of a term in a long lease because neither is the tenancy introductory, secure or assured, nor will the accommodation be provided under the relevant homelessness provisions (see section 153(4) of HA 1996).

Other powers

There is no reason why the powers outlined above (pp. 77-79) in relation to section 222 of LGA 1972 and taking action on behalf of others should not be employed against any owner-occupier and his or her family (whether or not the property was originally purchased from the landlord). Nonetheless in practice the courts are likely to be wary of granting injunctions which interfere with the exercise of an owner's property rights. For example, it is very unlikely that a court would make an order banning an owner-occupier from his or her home. The powers in section 152 of HA 1996 are confined to activities in and around dwellings held under local authority secure or introductory tenancies or provided by the authority under the relevant homelessness provisions (see section 152(1) and (2) of HA 1996 and p. 51, above). This would not seem to prevent action against perpetrators who are owner-occupiers, but in such a case the behaviour will have had to have been directed at the authority's tenants and their families and visitors, or others engaged in lawful activity around the authority's properties. In the case of noise or other behaviour which amounts to a statutory nuisance, it may be possible to obtain an injunction under section 81(5) of EPA 1990 see p. 52, above.

Case report

Croydon London Borough Council successfully obtained an interim injunction against an owner-occupier who under the terms of the injunction was banned from threatening, harassing and abusive behaviour, from playing amplified music and from shouting, screaming and making a general nuisance. The defendant was an owner-occupier of a maisonette who directed abuse, often racial, at other owner-occupiers and private tenants in the block. She would also deliberately play very loud music and make other noise. The injunction was obtained using the powers in section 222 of LGA 1972 and under the section 81(5) of EPA 1990. Following breach of the injunction the defendant was committed to six months imprisonment which was suspended for a year. *Croydon London Borough Council* (1997) (additional information kindly supplied by Croydon Tenancy Relations Officers).

Vulnerable perpetrators

Given the increasing number of people with mental health problems who are housed by social landlords it is perhaps not surprising that there should appear to be an increasing number of complaints of anti-social behaviour by such people. The perpetrator in this instance is often a tenant, although this is not always the case. In theory all the action which may be taken against a tenant (set out in Chapter 4), or against a non- tenant adult (set out above) will be available. In practice there are particular legal difficulties that may arise when seeking an injunction or possession against a vulnerable person and we now turn to these problems.

DETR Circular 2/97 sets out some of the particular difficulties that present themselves when dealing with vulnerable tenants. The advice is given in the context of introductory tenancies (but seems equally applicable to secure tenants) and is reiterated in DETR Environment Circular 12/97 in relation to seeking injunctions against vulnerable tenants:

> "Authorities must be vigilant to ensure that neighbours are not able to make a case for eviction against a vulnerable tenant whose behaviour may be different through no fault of that tenant's own. Such behaviour needs sympathetic handling by the authority and an understanding attitude from neighbours. Local authorities may need to set in place additional procedures to investigate complaints against vulnerable tenants." (paragraph 11)

> "Eviction is not necessarily appropriate when problems arise between a vulnerable tenant and neighbours. Where a vulnerable introductory tenant appears to have breached the terms of his tenancy, the landlord should liase with social services and other agencies to establish whether they are able to offer care or support services that might enable the tenant to remain." (paragraph 14)

It may be that the perpetrator's behaviour and state of health is so serious that for his or her own and others' protection he or she needs to be removed from the community. While it is always preferable that there is consent to treatment, if the perpetrator refuses there are powers under the Mental Health Act 1983 compulsorily to admit people to hospital. Applications for admission are usually made by an approved social worker. While we cannot in this book include a detailed discussion of this law, it is important that social landlords should be aware of the potential problems which tenants may have; they should know to whom they can turn if action needs to be taken. This requires proper channels of communication to be set up between the landlord and the relevant social services department. It also requires that issues of confidentiality be overcome. It is not unknown for social services departments to refuse to disclose any details of their clients to landlords, claiming that they are unable so to do. This is not the case. Confidentiality is not an absolute principle and must always be balanced against the wider needs of the public. Landlords and social workers need to work together and this includes disclosure of relevant information. Confidentiality problems can be overcome by working out proper protocols that define when and what information may be disclosed and to whom. Landlords should also ensure that where a tenant has an approved social worker that this is noted on file, with details of how he or she could be contacted.

Legal representation for perpetrator

When legal action is being considered the landlord must decide whether the proposed defendant's mental state is such that he or she can defend him or herself. If he or she is not in a position to do this, a guardian *ad litem* must to be appointed. Where the defendant already has a person appointed to manage his or her property and financial affairs under Part VII of the Mental Health Act 1983, that person can and should act as the guardian *ad litem*. Such appointments are dealt with by the Public Trust Office (at Stewart House, 24, Kingsway, London WC2B 6JX). Where no such person has been appointed then generally the plaintiff in the case (i.e. the landlord) must make an application to the court for an appointment. Where there is no one willing to act it is usually the Official Solicitor who is appointed. Where such an appointment is made the plaintiff must give the Official Solicitor an undertaking as to costs.

Injunctions

It is very unlikely that a court will grant an injunction against a defendant who is unable to understand it. When seeking an injunction against a perpetrator with mental health problems, is important to have available medical evidence that addresses this point.

Possession

Although possession may be sought on the usual basis, the fact that a perpetrator is vulnerable makes it less likely that possession will be granted because the judge is less likely to find it reasonable to grant possession.

Although when seeking eviction on the basis of nuisance and annoyance or breach of tenancy there is no requirement that suitable alternative accommodation be provided (see p. 70, above), it may help to show that it is reasonable to grant possession if such an offer is made. It may be, for example, that more suitable accommodation can be identified but the vulnerable tenant will not agree to a transfer. In these circumstances where possession is sought, the availability of the accommodation may persuade the judge that it is reasonable to grant possession.

The tenant's vulnerability should not, however, be considered as a complete bar on obtaining possession. Where there has been very serious anti-social behaviour the courts should start from the position that possession ought to be granted.

Case report

Mr Mousah was a tenant of Bristol City Council. Under the tenancy agreement, he covenanted not to supply drugs from the property. The covenant deemed the tenant to be responsible for breaches of the covenant by visitors to the property. On April and June 1994 the house was twice raided by the police and people arrested for possession of crack cocaine. The authority issued a notice of possession. Nevertheless, there was a further raid and arrest in August 1994. The authority commenced possession proceedings. Mr Mousah did not respond, and on 6 January 1995 he was ordered to file a defence by 27 January. He still did not respond, and an order was made that he would not be entitled to defend unless a defence was filed within 14 days. The defence was eventually filed on 3 May 1995.

At trial, in October 1995, the judge found that Mr Mousah was not involved in the crack cocaine dealing directly and had been away at the time it was going on. He found, however, that he was aware of the dealing, and on this basis was in breach of his tenancy agreement. Notwithstanding this he decided that it was not reasonable to make an order for possession. Evidence was given at the trial by Mr Mousah's consultant psychiatrist as to his schizophrenia. The psychiatrist said that the eviction would have a 'negative influence on his mental health'. On the basis of this the judge found that the public interest in not allowing the use of properties for drug dealing was outweighed by the public interest in keeping someone off the streets whose illness might cause him to become dangerous. Furthermore, the judge found that if he became homeless he would be dependent on the public sector to re-house him, but that the authority would probably find him intentionally homeless.

The Court of Appeal overturned this decision. The judge had misunderstood the evidence about Mr Mousah's health. There was no evidence that he would be a danger to the public or himself. Furthermore, while the judge was entitled to consider the effect of the order on the tenant he should not speculate on the outcome of any application to the authority as a homeless person. In relation to the delay although the last raid on the home had been many months before the trial, given much of the delay was due to the tenant failing to file his defence and given the seriousness of the conduct, this did not prevent it being reasonable to grant possession.
Bristol City Council v Mousah (1997)

Using environmental health powers

The nuisance caused by a vulnerable perpetrator may have some physical manifestation, such as the collection of rubbish or the failure to maintain a garden. In these circumstances it may be more appropriate to seek to use powers to deal with the physical problem, rather than preventing the behaviour through injunction or seeking eviction. The particular powers are considered in Chapter 6. Where environmental health powers are used against vulnerable perpetrators it may be better to use the powers in section 81(5) EPA 1990 (see p. 52, above), for example, to seek to remove rubbish rather than seek a criminal prosecution and fine or imprisonment.

6.
Specific Problems

Violence and drug dealing / Assaults on staff /
Noise / Rubbish / Pets / Cars

Specific types of nuisance and the action that can be taken to
prevent such problems are considered in this chapter.

Violence and drug dealing

Landlords will want to take firm action to deal with the most
serious conduct by tenants and their families and visitors.
Drug dealing on an estate can lead to a downward spiral
where existing tenants seek to move out and prospective
tenants refuse offers. Drug dealing often leads to violence
and other criminal activity, and where it is suspected,
co-operation with the police should be sought and swift, firm
action taken to prevent its occurrence.

Terms of tenancy

A common clause in tenancy agreements is that 'the tenant
must not use the dwelling house for illegal or immoral purposes, cause nuisance themselves or permit their families or
visitors to cause nuisance'. This covers violence and drug
dealing and indeed went further than Grounds 2 and 14
prior to their amendment (see p. 64, above). Yet it may well
be worth considering a clause that goes further than this.
It can be helpful for the clauses to set out very specifically

the types of behaviour that will not be tolerated. These may refer to violence and threatened violence, and also to the use of drugs on the premises. Thought should also be given to how wide a geographical area should be covered, and who should be protected (see further below on employees). Given the new Grounds 2 and 14 (see p. 64, above) the need for an extensive clause on violent conduct and drug dealing may not strictly be necessary to obtain possession. Nonetheless, setting out in clear detailed terms, in a document provided to the tenant at the outset of the tenancy, the conduct that will not tolerated will have two other benefits. It will help in obtaining an injunction based on breach of the tenancy agreement, and also in showing that it is reasonable to grant possession.

Injunctions

In matters involving criminal activities such as violence or drug dealing an application for an injunction, if supported with the appropriate affidavit evidence, is likely to stand a strong prospect of success. Clearly the balance of convenience will be strongly against permitting criminal acts. Where it is also possible that there will be a criminal prosecution some thought must, however, be given as to whether injunction proceedings are appropriate. In *Storrie v Southwark London Borough Council* (1997) (above p. 56) the Court of Appeal suggested that it may not be useful to launch injunction proceedings until at least a decision has been taken as to the first stage in criminal proceedings (i.e. whether the alleged perpetrator is to be arrested and charged). If injunction proceedings are taken and the per-petrator is then removed from the locality through arrest, the landlord should consider seeking a discharge of the injunction.

Possession

The new Grounds 2 and 14 are discussed in Chapter 4 above and should now address the most violent and criminal behaviour. As *Bristol City Council v Mousah* (1997) (p. 95, above) indicates it is only in exceptional cases that the courts will not grant outright possession.

Mousah was a Court of Appeal decision, but recent reports of county court decisions also show possession being granted. Thus, the London Borough of Camden evicted a tenant after complaints of harassment and of the fact that queues of prostitutes and drug dealers surrounded his flat (*Inside Housing*, 9 May 1997). Blythe Valley District Council evicted a tenant who permitted her partner to supply heroin from the premises: the court considered that the matter warranted an outright order for possession after 28 days (*Inside Housing*, 22 March 1996)

Assaults on staff

Terms of tenancy

Unfortunately there is an increasing number of incidents where housing officers are threatened and attacked and tenancy agreements should cover this situation. They should be widely drafted in order to cover attacks outside the locality of the tenant's home (which would come within the new Grounds 2 and 14) and ensure protection of staff wherever they are working. In local authorities consideration may also be given to including councillors amongst those who are protected.

Injunctions

Most cases involving threats of or actual violence can be dealt with by way of an *ex parte* application for an injunction in the first instance (see p. 54, above). It is important to remember that *ex parte* applications are only for cases of genuine urgency when there is no real possibility of giving notice. So it is important that there is no delay in making such an application. Even in cases where the application is on notice, cases may fail due to delay; an application which is made a month after an isolated incident will be undermined because the very lapse of time indicates that it is unlikely there will be any repetition of the behaviour.

The order is usually drafted in terms that the perpetrator is 'forbidden whether by themselves or any other person from assaulting, threatening or harassing' the victim. In some circumstances other terms may be necessary. If incidents have been linked to a specific locality such as a housing office an exclusion order may be appropriate. The Housing Act 1996 has extended the concept of locality (see Chapter 4) and assists in restricting access to certain areas on estates. However, it is important to remember that a tenant cannot be restricted from areas that provide essential access to his or her home; if this is required possession should be sought. Equally, if an injunction is granted against a tenant preventing him or her from coming to the local housing office, it will be important to make practical arrangements for complaints of disrepair and payment of rent.

Possession

If the tenancy agreement includes an appropriately worded term, acts of violence against staff can form the basis of a claim for possession. Prospects of success depend on the facts of the case and the evidence. In situations where an incident has been isolated it is unlikely that a judge would conclude that it was reasonable to make an order for possession, and undertakings or an application for an injunction may be more appropriate. However, in situations where there has been a concerted campaign against a particular member of staff or a series of attacks against a number of staff, an order for possession is likely. The principles are the same as that for an on-going nuisance by way of violence or noise. Camden London Borough Council evicted a tenant after she assaulted neighbours and threatened and abused council staff over a period of five years (*Inside Housing* 9 May 1997).

The amended definition of nuisance as set out in the Housing Act 1996 should assist local authorities in actions for possession founded upon abuse of employees. The definition of conduct is extended to behaviour which is 'likely to cause a nuisance' which will counter arguments that council officers are less likely to be affected by certain types of behaviour.

Criminal offences

Threats and acts of violence are criminal acts and the police should be involved where such incidents occur. Prosecution cannot, however, be guaranteed and is at the discretion of the Crown Prosecution Service (CPS). If the CPS chooses not to prosecute it is possible to launch a private prosecution, although this is likely to be expensive. Public sector landlords may wish to support staff in such actions, financially and in other ways. Where perpetrators are convicted of assaults on staff, such cases should be publicised in order to act as deterrents.

Noise

As well as being caused by anti-social behaviour, noise problems may also be the fault of the landlord (for example because of inadequate soundproofing). This is dealt with in Chapter 2 above where we consider whether the noise nuisance is the landlord's responsibility. Here we deal with the question of what action may be taken where the noise is the tenant's responsibility.

Terms of tenancy

Noise is usually part of a general clause obliging tenants not to cause a nuisance to their neighbours. However, clauses can be more specific by restricting noise at certain times, for example banning loud music being played during the hours of 11 pm and 7 am. They should also make it clear that unreasonable noise at any time is a nuisance.

Injunctions

It is possible to obtain an injunction to prevent noise nuisance. Common allegations are of shouting, fighting and loud music, although car alarms and barking dogs are increasingly becoming the subject of complaint. The evidence of environmental health officers, particularly those involved in noise patrols, is crucial in such cases and liaison between the environmental health department and housing officers will be important.

Landlords may become aware that a party is going to be held at a particular property, and may seek an injunction prior to its occurrence. In such cases, the application for an injunction is only likely to succeed if there has been more than one incident, or there is reason to believe that there will be repetition, or the party is professionally organised, such as a rave party.

Possession

The majority of applications for possession on the basis of nuisance contain some aspect of noise nuisance. In the event that the allegations are established, it is unlikely that the court will refuse to make an order for possession, although it may be prepared to suspend any order for possession in circumstances where the perpetrator may cease to cause the nuisance. Where there is evidence of repeated warnings being breached, however, an outright order will be appropriate (see *Leicester District Council v Blake* (1997) p. 81 above).

Prosecutions under EPA 1990

Noise nuisance can also be controlled though environmental legislation. Environmental health officers employed by local authorities generally take such action. It is important for social landlords (whether or not also the local authority) to be aware of such actions as the evidence may be useful in an action for possession.

By section 79(1)(g) of EPA 1990 statutory nuisance includes 'noise emitted from premises so as to be prejudicial to health or a nuisance'. By section 79(1)(g) a further definition is provided of 'noise that is prejudicial to health or a nuisance and is emitted from or caused by a vehicle, machinery or equipment in a street . . .' (e.g. where works are being carried out to cars on the street).

Section 79 places local authorities under a general duty to inspect their area from time to time in order to detect statutory nuisances and they are under a specific duty to investigate complaints. Where there is a noise nuisance, section 80(1) of EPA 1990 provides that the authority may serve an abatement notice on the person responsible or, if that person cannot be found, by fixing the notice onto the vehicle or machinery. Section 80(5) enables the person responsible to appeal against the notice by way of a hearing in the magistrates' court. The procedure at such hearings is considered in Chapter 8 below.

Section 81(3) of EPA 1990 provides the local authority with powers to abate the nuisance and section 81(4) to recover the expenses incurred in abating the nuisance from the person responsible. It is a defence to an abatement notice to show that the noise was authorised by a notice under section 60 or consent under section 61 of the Control of Pollution Act 1974 but this is very unlikely to be the case in relation to noise emanating from residential premises. Breach of an abatement notice can lead to a fine. One perpetrator was ordered to pay £2,700 for playing loud music and singing in breach of an abatement notice (*Inside Housing*, 7 June 1996).

Noise Act 1996

The Noise Act (NA) 1996 creates an offence of excessive noise at night from a dwelling and imposes a duty on local authorities to investigate such complaints. 'Night' is defined as the hours between 11 pm and 7 am. and the duty to investigate, set out in section 2, arises upon receipt of a complaint.

Section 2(4) of NA 1996 provides that the test for the officer conducting the investigation is whether the noise, if measured from the complainant's dwelling, would or may exceed the permitted level of decibels. If satisfied that the noise emitted from the dwelling during night hours would or may exceed the permitted level the officer may serve a warning notice, pursuant to section 3, that the person responsible may be guilty of an offence. The notice must specify a period for compliance of not less then 10 minutes after the service of the notice and ending the following 7am. By section 3(3) the notice must state the time of service and should be served on the person responsible. Anyone present or near the dwelling whom the officer of the authority considers to be responsible for the noise can be served. If this is not practicable, the notice can be left at the offending dwelling. The definition of the 'person responsible' is similar to that in the Environmental Protection Act 1990, namely the person 'by whose act default or sufferance the emission of the noise is wholly or partly attributable'.

Section 8 enables the officer to serve a fixed penalty notice if he has reasonable cause to believe that an offence is being committed under section 4 (i.e. if a notice is not complied with). A fixed penalty notice enables the offender to discharge liability of conviction of the offence by payment of a fixed penalty. The penalty is £100 and if this is paid within 14 days a prosecution cannot be brought.

Section 10 enables the officer to seize equipment that it appears to him has been used in the emission of the noise where a warning notice has been served and excessive noise has been emitted during the period specified in the notice. The equipment may be retained for 28 days or until criminal proceedings are resolved unless a fixed penalty notice has been given and paid.

If a person is convicted of an offence under the Noise

Act 1996 the court may order forfeiture of the equipment but must have regard to its value and the financial effect on the offender. Within six months of forfeiture the owner may apply to the court for its return. The court must be satisfied that the owner did not consent to the offender having the equipment and did not know or have reason to suspect that it would be likely to be used in the commission of an offence. In the event that the authority considers that the person in whose case forfeiture was made was not the owner, it is under a duty to take reasonable steps to notify persons who may be entitled to apply.

Rubbish

Rubbish collecting in the dwelling, the garden or in common parts can become a nuisance and a health hazard. It may often be a problem caused by elderly or vulnerable tenants, in which case careful consideration should be given to alternative avenues before legal steps are taken.

Terms of tenancy

Tenancy agreements usually include a clause obliging the tenant not to litter the commons parts. A well-drafted agreement will oblige the tenant to keep communal passages, balconies, gardens and yards free of rubbish. However, many tenancy agreements contain a widely drafted provision obliging the landlord 'in so far as is practicable to keep the common parts of the estate clean and tidy'. The tenancy agreement should make it clear where the tenants' obligations begin and the landlord's end.

Injunctions and possession

Given the above example of a tenancy agreement, the landlord should be able to enforce the tenancy conditions by way of an action for possession and/or a claim for an injunction. However, the tenant can equally enforce any breach of the landlord's covenants by way of an action for damages or an injunction. If the obligation on the landlord is limited by the terms such as 'where reasonable' or 'so far as practicable' it is only in the case of a clear breach that such an action by the tenant will succeed.

Environmental Protection Act and other powers

By section 79(1)(e) of EPA 1990 a statutory nuisance includes 'any accumulation which is prejudicial to health or a nuisance'. This can lead to an abatement notice as with noise (see above). Where a vulnerable tenant is involved it may be appropriate for the authority to use its powers to abate the nuisance itself.

Pets

While the keeping of pets may be a perfectly innocent – and indeed therapeutic – activity, on some occasions it may become a nuisance, particularly when animals are kept in excessive numbers. Furthermore some animals, particularly dogs, may be used in violent or threatening behaviour against tenants or staff.

Terms of tenancy

Most tenancy agreements prevent tenants from keeping pets or limit the number of pets that can be kept in one property. Some agreements prohibit tenants from keeping certain types of animal: particular consideration needs to be given to whether dogs should be permitted at all, and if so whether their numbers should be limited. It may also be thought appropriate to prevent the keeping of potentially dangerous animals such as poisonous snakes. Even if not banned outright, the tenancy agreement may require permission to be sought before certain types of pets are allowed. If this is the case it is important to have the appropriate administrative machinery, which also provides for consistent decision-making. Where pets are permitted tenants should always be required to keep them in such a manner that they do not cause a nuisance, and be required to prevent them fouling communal areas. The possibility of disease caused by dog mess in children's play areas is a particular problem. It is important that, where terms are included which limit the right to keep pets, they are consistently enforced, as tenants will very quickly complain if they are being asked to comply when neighbours are not.

Injunctions

The landlord can apply for an injunction to enforce the terms of the tenancy. The form of injunction sought clearly depends on the nature of the problem, but in the case of an outright ban an injunction should be granted.

Case report

The defendant, Mr Lawrence, who was suffering from multiple sclerosis, kept a dog as a companion, in breach of tenancy conditions. His landlord, Sutton Housing Trust, applied for an order removing the dog and an injunction restraining him from keeping a dog in future. The judge refused the injunction on the basis that committal was unlikely and the Trust had an alternative remedy, namely possession proceedings. However, he made a declaration that Mr Lawrence was prohibited from keeping a dog at the premises. The Trust appealed. The appeal was upheld on the basis that the fact it was unlikely that committal proceedings would be sought or granted was not relevant, nor was it relevant that the Trust had an alternative remedy by way of possession proceedings.

Sutton Housing Trust v Lawrence (1987)

Possession

Possession can be sought under Grounds 1 and 2 of HA 1985 or 12 or 14 of HA 1988 for breach of tenancy conditions and/or nuisance. Where a tenant refuses to comply with the conditions, such a claim is normally successful and it is only in exceptional cases that a continuing breach of tenancy conditions will not lead to an order for possession, possibly suspended on terms.

Case reports

Ms Jepson was a secure tenant of Sheffield City Council and, in breach of tenancy conditions, kept a dog in the premises. The council sought possession. Evidence was given of nuisance in the block due to the presence of dogs. The judge refused to order possession on the grounds that there was nothing in the evidence about the behaviour of Ms Jepson's dog that made it reasonable to make the order. On appeal it was found that there was no reasonable basis upon which the judge could find that the council had failed to prove it was reasonable to make an order. The breach was deliberate and persistent and the making of complaints showed other tenants were caused a nuisance.
Sheffield City Council v Jepson (1993)

*

In breach of covenant Mr Green kept a dog, initially because he felt it would protect his wife against the Yorkshire Ripper. The couple divorced and the defendant continued to keep the dog in the premises. A suspended order for possession was granted and was upheld by the Court of Appeal; the emergency occasioned by the activities of the Yorkshire Ripper was over and there was no evidence before the judge that could support the exercise of his discretion in favour of the defendant.
Green v Sheffield City Council (1994)

Other powers

Some tenants may use a dog, particularly those which are perceived to be aggressive, to threaten other tenants or council officials. Such action may in itself constitute a criminal offence, such as assault or breach of the Public Order Acts, and could result in prosecution.

There is also a number of Acts that deal specifically with the keeping of dogs. The Dogs Act 1871 provides that if a court considers a dog to be dangerous and not kept under proper control it may order the owner to keep the dog under proper control or to destroy it. The Dangerous Dogs Act 1989 gives the court the power to disqualify an owner from having custody of a dog for the period specified. Where the owner fails to comply with an order pursuant to section 2 of the Dogs Act 1871 to keep the dog under proper control or deliver it up for destruction, he or she is guilty of an offence under the Dangerous Dogs Act 1989 and may be fined.

The Dangerous Dogs Act 1991 applies to certain breeds of dog, including the Pitt Bull terrier and the Japanese Tosa. It imposes restrictions such that the dogs must be muzzled and kept on a lead in a public place. It is an offence to breed, sell, abandon or give away as a gift such an animal. Breach of the Act carries a fine or a maximum penalty of six months' imprisonment.

The Dogs Fouling of Land Act 1996 creates an offence of allowing a dog to defecate on designated land to which the public has access (as defined by the local authority). Where housing estates include play areas and other public open space it is appropriate to seek to have these designated. Under the Act and the Dogs Fouling (Fixed Penalties) Order 1996 (SI 1996 No. 2763), fines may be levied on those who permit dogs to foul in public places.

There are cases where aggressive behaviour or loud barking may be symptomatic of abuse from the animal's owner. There are occasions when the most appropriate action is to involve voluntary organisations such as the

RSPCA, which has a wide range of powers including prosecution of owners and confiscation of animals.

Cars

Terms of tenancy

Cars can form a particular problem. A well-drafted tenancy agreement will provide for some or all of the following:
1. parking is only permitted in designated areas;
2. the tenant may only park in a space or garage rented from the council;
3. only vehicles within specified dimensions can be parked;
4. the tenant must not carry out motor vehicle repairs which in the landlord's view are or may be a nuisance;
5. the tenant shall not permit members of his or her family or visitors to park other than as designated;
6. the landlord is permitted to wheel-clamp or tow away vehicles which are not within the designated areas or which are causing an obstruction and to recover the costs incurred.

Injunctions and possession

The landlord could seek an injunction to enforce the terms of tenancy and possession for breach of Ground 1 of HA 1985 and, where appropriate, Ground 2 and the equivalent grounds in the 1988 Act.

> **Case report**
>
> The defendants were secure tenants of a house owned by the plaintiffs. In breach of tenancy conditions the defendants kept a caravan in their front garden and the plaintiffs sought possession. The defendants had applied for permission from the plaintiffs to keep the caravan but permission was

> refused on the grounds that as a matter of policy
> permission was never granted. The second de-
> fendant was severely disabled. The judge's decision
> that it was not reasonable to grant an order for pos-
> session because of the policy was considered to be a
> misdirection. The policy was not a factor relevant to
> the question of reasonableness.
> *Barking & Dagenham London Borough Council v Hyatt
> and Hyatt* (1991)

Criminal offences and other action

Roads on an estate are commonly private, and are owned by the landlord. However certain acts may constitute criminal offences. Problems with joy-riding on estates are problematic as they are not occurring on public roads. On the whole the problems are now addressed by speed humps and certain actions are likely to constitute criminal damage or breach of the Public Order Acts.

The Refuse Disposal (Amenity) Act 1978 creates an offence of abandoning a motor vehicle, or part of one on a public road. The authority can remove the vehicle and the perpetrator can be fined or imprisoned for a maximum of three months.

7.
Behaviour Motivated by Race and Other Prejudices

Terms of tenancy / Duties to combat racism / Injunctions and possession

For some perpetrators of anti-social behaviour the victim's identity is neither here nor there – he or she just happens to be in the wrong place at the wrong time. For others, however, the victim can be targeted because of his or her particular attributes – be it race, gender, sexual orientation, disability or old age. Such behaviour is particularly distressing for the victims and requires very sensitive treatment. We shall in this chapter refer to such behaviour as 'motivated harassment'.

The failure of landlords to act against perpetrators, particularly of racial harassment, was criticised extensively in the late 1980s and early 1990s (see e.g. *Making the Law Work Against Racial Harassment*, Legal Action Group, 1990). Many landlords, however, have in more recent years taken on a more active commitment in such cases. Furthermore there seems to be greater evidence of success. Thus in the year to May 1996 a London Housing Unit survey found that 16 of London's 33 councils had taken action against racially abusive tenants. A total of 14 possession orders and 43 injunctions had been obtained. Nonetheless, it is clear that some landlords are still failing to protect their tenants. For example, in 1997 the Housing Association Ombudsman found that Springboard Housing Association had failed to protect a couple from five years of racial harassment.

It is important that landlords have clear policies in relation to such behaviour. Assistance in formulating such a strategy and in training staff may be obtained from G. Lemos, C. Hunter and C. Foreman *How to Tackle Racial Harassment in Housing*, Lemos & Crane (forthcoming) and *Tackling discrimination against lesbians and gay men*, NFHA, 1994.

In some ways the law does not look any differently on the behaviour just because it has a particular motivation, and all that has been said above in Chapters 4 and 5 in relation to obtaining possession and injunctions will apply in cases where the conduct has a particular motivation. The issues which are considered in this chapter are the specific terms which may be included in the tenancy to deal with such behaviour; particular responsibilities in relation to racially motivated attacks; and obtaining injunctions and possession in cases of prejudicially motivated behaviour.

Terms of tenancy

A tenancy that is drawn widely enough to cover nuisance and annoyance to neighbours and others should cover behaviour that constitutes motivated harassment. Some tenancy agreements, however, have sought to spell out what they mean by harassment. For example some include a specific definition of harassment, which the tenant, other members of the household and visitors must not commit. One definition from D. Forbes *Action on Racial Harassment*, Legal Action Group, 1988, which has been adopted by a number of social landlords is:

"Harassment includes but is not limited to:
(a) violence or threats of violence towards any person;
(b) abusive or insulting words or behaviour;
(c) damage or threats of damage to property belonging to another person including damage to any part of a person's home;

(d) writing threatening, abusive or insulting graffiti;
(e) any act or omission calculated to interfere with the peace or comfort of any person or to inconvenience such person."

Once defined it is made clear to tenants what behaviour will not be tolerated, and puts some flesh on the bones of the rather nebulous concepts of 'nuisance and annoyance'. The question which landlords may want to address is whether anti-harassment clauses need to be linked specifically to motivated harassment. In a sense it does not matter why harassment takes place: in any circumstances landlords wish to prevent such conduct by their tenants. Forbes' clause seeks to prevent 'harassment (whether racial, sexual or otherwise)'. It may well be important to send a message to tenants in their tenancy agreement that motivated harassment will not be tolerated. But it is also important to recognise the difficulties of proving particular motivation. While it is sometimes very obvious (e.g. because of the language used by the perpetrator that the behaviour was motivated by racism or homophobia) at other times there may be no direct evidence of why a particular victim was targeted. It is much easier to prove in court that the conduct took place than to prove why it took place.

It is therefore important that tenancy clauses do not in any way limit themselves only to actions where the motivation can be proved. This is not to say that they should not contain explicit reference to such behaviour, but they need to ensure that they are drawn widely enough to catch the behaviour whatever its motivation. The fact that attention is drawn to motivation will add weight to the case that it is reasonable to make an outright order for possession (see below).

Duties in relation to racism

While it is good practice to have proper policies to deal with all motivated harassment, local authorities and registered social landlords must consider their policies on racial harassment in the light of specific statutory duties.

Section 71 of the Race Relations Act imposes an obligation on local authorities to eliminate unlawful discrimination and 'to promote equality of opportunity and good race relations'. Authorities who fail to make appropriate arrangements to deal with racial harassment could be in breach of this duty (see further Chapter 2 above). Section 71 also applies to the Housing Corporation and Tai Cymru (the Housing Corporation for Wales) (section 75(5) of the Housing Associations Act 1985). They must seek to eliminate unlawful discrimination and promote equality of opportunity in all their functions, including the supervision of registered social landlords.

The question of whether breach of these duties gives rise to a cause of action against a local authority in the case of racial harassment is considered in Chapter 2 at p. 33, above.

Injunctions and possession

Whether injunctions or possession are sought against the perpetrators of motivated harassment, the same law is applicable as in other cases of anti-social behaviour (see Chapters 4 and 5 above). Some specific points may, however, be worth raising in this context.

Injunctions

The Public Order Act 1986 creates a number of offences in connection with racial hatred. Section 4A(1) makes it an offence to use threatening, abusive or insulting words or behaviour, or disorderly behaviour, or display any writing, sign or other visible representation which is threatening, abusive or insulting with intent to cause – and which thereby does cause – a person harassment, alarm or distress. The offence may be committed in both public and private places, although not if the perpetrator and victim are both inside dwellings. Generally prosecution is a matter for the CPS. The existence of the crime, however, may be combined with action under section 222 of LGA 1972 (see p. 77, above) by local authorities to take out injunction proceedings against perpetrators (e.g. banning them from a particular area). Further criminal offences of racial harassment have been created by the Crime and Disorder Act, which may also form the basis of action under section 222.

The taking of successful action (including imprisonment for contempt) is illustrated by the following case, although it is not clear from the brief report on what legal basis the injunction was obtained.

Case report

The London Borough of Southwark obtained an injunction against Mr Byrne banning him from a particular area and acting in an intimidatory way following a number of incidents of racial harassment. Following a vicious attack on three Somali youths the court was satisfied that Mr Byrne was present in the street at the time and was in breach of the injunction. The High Court imprisoned him for two months for contempt.
Southwark London Borough Council v Byrne **(1996)**

Possession

There has been an increasing number of examples of successful claims for possession based on racial harassment in the housing press, and in the case of *Kensington & Chelsea Royal Borough Council v Simmonds* (1996) (p. 88, above) the Court of Appeal upheld a suspended order for possession where the behaviour of the tenant's son was racially motivated. Where there is evidence of motivated harassment this should always be included as part of the pleadings and evidence. Courts should take this into account as an aggravating factor which makes it more reasonable to grant possession.

Overtly racist conduct, which includes publishing and distributing written racist material contrary to section 19 of the Public Order Act 1986, is an arrestable offence that could then lead to possession under the new Ground 2 of HA 1985 or Ground 14 of HA 1988. The new offence of racially aggravated harassment in the Crime and Disorder Act is also designated an arrestable offence.

8.

Procedure and Problems at Court

Civil proceedings / Criminal proceedings

Many aspects of housing law involve compromise and settlement, disrepair being a prime example. However, matters involving nuisance invariably involve the need for at least a preliminary hearing (such as an application for an injunction) and frequently proceed to trial. Furthermore, nuisance cases can involve certain difficulties regarding evidence. This chapter addresses the procedure and difficulties that can occur at trial, whether it be civil proceedings for an injunction or possession, or criminal proceedings under the environmental health legislation or other powers.

Civil proceedings

Injunction proceedings

It is common in cases involving nuisance to seek injunctive relief at an early stage. Evidence is given on affidavit as part of pending proceedings. It is important to have affidavit evidence from those who have witnessed the incidents. Where the matter concerns behaviour on the common parts of an estate it is useful to have an affidavit from a senior housing officer outlining the nature of the disturbance (e.g. vandalism or drug dealing) and the number of complaints received.

Any documents (such as the conditions of tenancy) or other evidence (e.g. video surveillance equipment) should be exhibited to the affidavit. The person who took the photos or shot the video should preferably make the affidavit. If this is not possible, the affidavit should state who did take the photos and how they were passed to the person swearing the affidavit. Material that is not exhibited to an affidavit cannot be relied on in the application. It may be useful in cases involving serious criminal behaviour, where the court is being asked to exclude perpetrators from the estate, to include a general affidavit from a senior officer in the housing department which describes generally the effect of the behaviour on the estate. This scene-setting description could cover the general level of complaints from residents, requests for transfers, void rates and lost rents. It could also usefully set out a history of the estate. Such an affidavit allows the judge to see the bigger picture and be aware that the case is not simply about disputes between a limited number of residents. On the contrary, it has an impact on the whole estate, and indeed, in local authorities, on all council tenants through the impact on the Housing Revenue Account.

Breach of an injunction can lead to committal proceedings and the court has the power to fine or imprison the perpetrator (see p. 62). Evidence at the committal hearing will be from witnesses, under oath. It is necessary to prove the breach to a criminal standard (i.e. beyond reasonable doubt).

Procedure and evidence at trial

Procedure in a civil trial is as follows:
1. The plaintiff opens the case.
2. The plaintiff calls witnesses.
3. The defendant calls witnesses.
4. The defendant's closing speech.
5. The plaintiff's closing speech.
6. The judgment.

Pleadings

Claims for possession are brought in the county court. A claim or a defence to a claim cannot be based upon matters that are not pleaded. Pleadings should contain all the facts on which the claim is based. The following are essential.

Particulars of Claim   This document should set out the following details:

1. The parties and their relationship (e.g. 'the plaintiff is a local authority landlord and the defendant is a secure tenant').
2. The relevant terms of the tenancy agreement in full and the grounds on which possession is sought, usually Grounds 1 and 2 of Schedule 2 to HA 1985 in the case of secure tenancies, or Grounds 12 and 14 of Schedule 2 to HA 1988 for assured tenants.
3. If reliance is to be made on nuisance as a cause of action, it must be pleaded.
4. Particulars of all incidents relied upon should be given. In many cases the incidents may be numerous and a schedule can be annexed to the Particulars of Claim, although this should be referred to in the body of the pleading.
5. The date and method of service of any notice of seeking possession or notice to quit should be pleaded.
6. Any attempts to negotiate or prevent the nuisance should be pleaded. (In the event that the court is considering suspending any order for possession, this may persuade the judge that there are no grounds for doing so.)
7. The relief sought should be clearly stated; possession should be claimed, as well as damages, if appropriate, and damages for use and occupation from the date of the order for possession until the date of possession. If damages for use and occupation are not pleaded they cannot be claimed.

8. In noise nuisance cases an acoustic expert's report may be obtained. It is good practice, but not essential, to annex such a report to the pleadings.
9. In a claim for damages against a landlord for noise nuisance resulting from structural defects (see Chapter 2) the action is likely to involve a claim for personal injury. The claim is likely to be of stress and mental anguish, although it could be for physical injury. In order to advance a claim for personal injury a medical report must be annexed to the particulars of claim (CCR 1981 Order 6 Rule 1 (5)(a)).

Defence   The defences in a claim for nuisance are limited. The following should be included, where appropriate:

1. The landlord should be put to strict proof of the service of any notice of seeking possession or notice to quit.
2. If a version of events which is contrary to that pleaded is to be the defence, it should be set out fully. If the complainant has put forward the allegations on the basis of a grudge, or is a family member or former friend, this should be pleaded.
3. In the event the defendant is a landlord and the basis of the claim is a structural defect and evidence to the contrary is available, it is good practice to annex such reports to the defence.
4. In a defence to a claim for personal injury it is good practice to annex any medical report showing that the plaintiff has not suffered as alleged to the defence.
5. If the defendant is an addict and has entered rehabilitation, details should be set out. On occasions the defendant may have caused a nuisance prior to being treated but has then ceased to cause problems. If this is the case it may be sufficient to persuade a court to refuse the application for possession or, more probably, to find grounds that it is reasonable to suspend any order for possession. Medical evidence in support is vital evidence and may be annexed to the pleadings.

Gathering evidence

The following suggestions apply equally to all cases of nuisance, but can be of particular assistance in serious and complicated cases. Social landlords may well have the resources to undertake the following; however, limited funding coupled with an increasing number of complaints means that it is neither possible nor necessary to undertake all of the following in every case.

Professional witnesses

Surveillance by professional investigators can be extremely useful and is an increasingly common method of supporting allegations. The evidence of the professional detective can mean that it will not be necessary for victims to give evidence in court. Such schemes have been successful because witnesses who had fears of reprisals were reassured by contact with a professional witness who was on call day and night. When setting up a professional witness scheme care needs to be taken: they can be very expensive. It is important to use those with the necessary expertise – people who are properly accredited with an appropriate professional body. Potential cases must be carefully identified: What evidence is the professional witness to collect? What are the chances of him or her actually witnessing the behaviour? What steps need to be taken to ensure that perpetrators are unaware of the presence of the professional witness? Clearly, moving a single man into a three-bedroomed house may well arouse suspicions that he is not an ordinary tenant. A number of authorities including Chesterfield Borough Council and Sunderland City Council have introduced a professional witness scheme for appropriate cases.

Case report

**Allegations that a tenant of Nottingham City
Council and her family were involved in vandalism,
criminal damage, verbal abuse, racist intimidation,
burglary and theft were made. The council employed
two private detectives. They posed as a couple
moving into a nearby home and were able to obtain
overwhelming evidence within a few days. Their
evidence was crucial in obtaining an outright possession order. (*Inside Housing*, 3 May 1996.)**

Video cameras

Installation of a video camera can serve as a deterrent to the
perpetrators if obvious, but can be hidden and act as compelling evidence, provided the pictures are clear enough to
identify individual perpetrators.

Diaries

Diaries should be provided to all potential witnesses. Those
who have not wished to become involved may be more
likely to note incidents if it is easy to do so. Hounslow
London Borough Council evicted a tenant with the assistance of detailed diaries kept by residents (*Inside Housing*
26 April 1996). Diaries should include the date, the time, the
nature of the incident, the names of those involved and the
action taken. It is important for landlords to keep control
over diary evidence: diary sheets should not be sprayed
around like confetti. To provide useful evidence landlords
should date stamp them on handing them out, and also have
a system for their collection. This should occur at regular
intervals (ideally weekly). They should then be date stamped
on their return. Taking these steps ensures that the diaries
can be shown to be a contemporary record of what occurred.

The police

Liaison with the police can be extremely helpful. Police witnesses are likely to be regarded as witnesses of truth and in cases where there is a serious conflict in the evidence are likely to be crucial. It is important to remember that many acts of anti-social behaviour and nuisance are crimes, commonly breaches of the Public Order Acts, assault or criminal damage. Those who are willing to be witnesses in civil proceedings are likely to be willing to give evidence in criminal proceedings. If the CPS chooses to prosecute and is successful, this may alleviate the problem if a sentence of imprisonment is imposed and will also be compelling evidence in possession proceedings.

It is not uncommon for the perpetrators of nuisance to be known to the police. The perpetrator may be on bail for other offences and committing an offence while on bail is likely to constitute a breach of the conditions of bail and could lead to bail being revoked. Housing officers should encourage victims to contact the police immediately if violence or threats of violence are involved. The recent high profile of nuisance and anti-social behaviour has encouraged an increased police involvement and beat officers in particular may be prepared to take an active role in a particular case.

Witness protection

It is a commonly held view that many cases collapse because witnesses refuse to give evidence. While this is undoubtedly the case in some instances, there are many steps that landlords can take to seek to avert this happening. It is important that witnesses are not put off from the outset by being told that they 'have to give evidence'. They should be encouraged to report incidents come what may and appropriate steps should be taken to obtain evidence from other sources (e.g. professional witnesses) if tenants are genuinely being intimidated.

A number of policies can be introduced to encourage victims to pursue cases. These may include:

1. the provision of safety measures in the home (e.g. grilles)
2. the provision of an alarm system, similar to that provided by many social landlords for elderly people;
3. a clear transfer policy.

This latter can present a difficult balance. On the one hand, to permit transfers where intimidatory behaviour is taking place, particularly where it is motivated by prejudice, is to give the perpetrators what they are seeking. On the other, it is unfair to refuse to transfer those who may be living in enormous fear. What needs to be fostered is an attitude that a transfer is not an end to the matter. Those who are transferred should be encouraged to continue to participate in legal proceedings.

There is also a number of legal steps which can be taken to protect witnesses. In particular the Protection from Harassment Act 1997 may be used where there has been harassment of particular witnesses. Section 1 of the Act creates an offence of 'harassment' which is committed when a person harasses another and knows or ought to know that the conduct amounts to harassment. In addition to the criminal offence created, where harassment has occurred or is apprehended the victim may also bring civil proceedings (section 3). Such proceedings may include an application for an injunction restraining the perpetrator from pursuing any conduct that amounts to harassment. Landlords may wish to consider funding such applications (see p. 78, above) where particular witnesses are being targeted by perpetrators.

Presenting evidence

Notice of seeking possession

The Housing Act 1996 greatly assisted landlords in overcoming a common problem in proceedings for possession.

Previously the landlord was required to prove service of a notice of seeking possession. A common problem was caused when officers who had served the notice left the employment of the local authority or housing association and could not be traced. The Act provides that the court can dispense with the requirements of the notice where it considers it just and equitable to do so (section 83 of HA 1985, as amended by the HA 1996). There has always been equivalent provision in the HA 1988 (see section 8(1)(b)).

Actions started prior to the commencement of the Act still require proof of the service of the notice. Without such evidence, regardless of the merits, the action will fail. Clearly the problem will lessen with time.

However, there are occasions in nuisance actions when a case may be adjourned generally with liberty to restore, by consent, on the basis that a nuisance has ceased. Such situations are most common in relation to perpetrators who are addicts who have entered a rehabilitation programme, but then lapse. In such cases it is important to remember that an application to restore the action will fall under the provisions prior to the Act. Therefore, serious consideration should be given to discontinuing the old action and commencing fresh proceedings; clearly this is essential if the person who served the notice seeking possession is not available to give evidence.

Witness statements

The procedure in the county court means that the main evidence of the witnesses for either side is given in a witness statement. This then stands as the witness's evidence-in-chief. A witness statement is a document setting out the evidence to be given by the witness and which must be signed and dated. It is then served on the other party by way of mutual exchange of witness statements. Supplementary evidence may be allowed by the trial judge and often is relied upon in nuisance cases in order to update the court of any incidents which have occurred after the statements were exchanged.

Such evidence will bear on the question of whether it is reasonable to make an order for possession at all or whether any order that is made should be suspended.

The fact that the trial judge has discretion to allow supplementary evidence should not mean that relevant material is excluded from witness statements. It is of vital importance that witnesses inform their advisers of all matters at the stage when statements are being drafted, even those which they may consider of little relevance or adverse to their case.

If important information is excluded from such statements the judge is entitled to refuse to allow such evidence to be relied upon, which in an extreme case could prove fatal to the case. The alternative may be to offer the other party the chance of an adjourned hearing in order to file further witness statements in response, and it is likely that the costs of the hearing would be borne by the defaulting party.

The complainant may not be the only victim of the nuisance. Family, neighbours and friends may also be victims or have witnessed certain incidents. A reluctant complainant may well feel less isolated if others are prepared to give evidence. Housing officers or contractors may be present when an incident occurred. In the most serious cases it is worth considering tracing passers-by through advertisements in local papers or posters. Records of those who have sought transfers away from a particular neighbourhood may also yield further witnesses.

Many disputes lead to counter allegations being made. Once a decision has been taken to act notwithstanding such allegations, it is important to obtain as much corroborative evidence as possible. Where there is simply an allegation and a counter allegation a judge is unlikely to make an order for possession.

Civil Evidence Act 1995

Hearsay evidence is that given by a witness who does not have direct knowledge of the evidence. An example is where a housing officer, who did not witness an incident, is able to give evidence of the complaint that the victim made to him or her about the incident, such as notes in a diary. Hearsay evidence is permitted in affidavits in interim injunctions (see p. 53 above), and since the coming into force of the Civil Evidence Act 1995 it has also been permitted at final trial. Section 1 of the Act enables parties to adduce hearsay evidence. By section 2 the party is required to give such notice and particulars of the evidence as is reasonable or practicable in the circumstance. The court has a wide discretion over the weight to be given to such evidence (see section 4).

The Act is likely to provide considerable assistance in cases involving anti-social behaviour. It should be remembered, however, that if evidence is in dispute and is central to the case the party calling oral evidence is likely to be at an advantage, since hearsay evidence is accorded less weight than the direct evidence of witnesses to a particular incident. The Act does not, therefore, mean that oral evidence from witnesses is not necessary. The judge needs to be persuaded that on the balance of probabilities the conduct took place. Before launching any possession action landlords must consider with their lawyers whether their evidence will match up to this standard. Hearsay evidence, in the form of diaries and photographs, assisted in obtaining an order for possession by Broomleigh Housing Association against a tenant whose 13-year-old daughter terrorised neighbours (*Inside Housing*, 7 November 1997). Using such evidence, if it is compelling enough, without the victims having to come to court may persuade them to take part. Victims should not be told that unless they are willing to come to court 'nothing can be done'.

Criminal proceedings

When the Crime and Disorder Act is brought into force it is likely that local authorities will become much more closely involved in criminal prosecutions (e.g. for failure to comply with an anti-social behaviour order). For the moment, they are most likely to be encountered in the context of the Environmental Protection Act 1990. Actions under the 1990 Act do not fall within the magistrates' court civil jurisdiction. They are criminal in nature (*Botross v London Borough of Hammersmith & Fulham* (1994); *Davenport v Walsall Metropolitan Borough Council* (1995)) and the prosecution must therefore prove the case beyond all reasonable doubt. The procedure in a criminal trial, which would be the case where a tenant has failed to comply with an abatement notice under EPA 1990 (see p. 104, above) is as follows:

1. The prosecution opens the case.
2. The prosecution calls evidence.
3. At the close of the prosecution case the defence can submit that there is no case to answer.
4. The defendant calls evidence.
5. The defendant's closing speech.
6. The prosecution's right to reply solely on matters of law
7. The judgment.

Evidence

The relaxation of rules on hearsay evidence does not apply in the magistrates' court. Witnesses must give direct oral evidence unless one of the following steps have been taken:

Service of statement pursuant to Criminal Justice Act 1967, section 9

If the person receiving the notice does not serve a counter notice within the specified time of seven days, the statement is submitted as evidence and the other party can only require the witness to attend to give oral evidence with the leave of the court. However, the statement must be in the correct form and the party relying on the statement *must* produce the original of the statement to the court clerk at trial. The statement can be served in respect of the evidence of any witness, although is most commonly used to prevent additional costs of expert witnesses attending court. Unless a counter notice is served, or the court grants leave, the evidence is admissible and therefore such statements can also be useful in relation to nervous witnesses who may fail to attend court.

Admission pursuant to Criminal Justice Act 1967, section 10

This is a formal admission of a fact in issue. The admission must be in writing if made otherwise than at court and must be signed by the person making the admission; it must be made or approved by counsel or solicitor if the defendant is an individual.

Non-compliance with the formalities cannot be agreed by consent between the parties (e.g. if the original signed section 9 statement is not available), the statement is inadmissible.

Witnesses must remain outside court until they have given evidence. Breach may lead to their evidence being considered tainted and therefore of reduced weight or may lead to such evidence being excluded. The sole exception to this rule is the expert witness.

The only evidence which must be disclosed by both prosecution and defence are expert reports, which must be disclosed prior to trial. The defence is under no obligation to disclose any other evidence or the basis of the defence. Matters brought under the EPA 1990 are summary only and therefore the prosecution is not obliged to disclose the information upon which it relies.

Submission of no case to answer

The prosecution is obliged to prove each element of the offence. A submission of no case to answer can be made on the basis of either of the following:

1. The evidence adduced is so unworthy of belief that no tribunal properly directed could convict. In practice this submission is only appropriate when the evidence is clearly contradictory. Generally matters of credibility should be dealt with in the context of the burden of proof during the defence closing speech.
2. That the prosecution has failed to prove an essential element of the offence. Thus, for example, in an action under section 82 of EPA 1990 the proceedings are often taken against the owner pursuant to section 82(4)(b). Submissions of no case to answer have succeeded, at first instance, on the basis that no office copy of the land registry certificate has been produced (this being real evidence) and therefore the prosecution has failed to establish that ownership and they are proceedings against the correct defendant. Although such decisions are not binding upon other tribunals the certificate should be produced as a matter of caution.

Defences

In some cases a defendant (landlord) may accept that there is a nuisance for which he or she is responsible but the complainant (tenant) may be refusing access. This is a defence to this matter (*Warner v Lambeth London Borough Council* (1984) and *Carr v Hackney London Borough Council* (1996)). Such defences may be relevant in prosecutions against the landlord in cases where there is an allegation of noise nuisance resulting from poor insulation.

Index

OTHER RECENT TITLES IN ARDEN'S HOUSING LIBRARY

Rights to Buy and Acquire

Law and practice in the management of social housing
Josephine Henderson, Barrister

"This book will be essential reading and reference for any housing professional with the thankless task of administering sales to tenants... the step-by-step guide to procedures in Chapter 4 is worth the purchase price by itself." *Agenda*

Council and some housing assocation tenants have had the Right to Buy their homes for nearly 20 years. A new Right to Acquire has been introduced for the tenants of housing associations and other registered social landlords.

Meanwhile as problems surface from the early burst of sales activity in the 1980s an accessible guide to the legal process that underpins these rights has been lacking. This book fills the gap.

Contents include:

Who has the Right to Buy? • Qualifications and Exceptions • What is Bought?
• Procedure • The Price and Paying It • The Grant or Conveyance
• Loss and Enforcement of Right to Buy • Changes in the Landlord's Interest
• Extension of Right • Housing Associations and Other Registered Social Landlords

1997   ISBN 1-898001-15-4

Leaseholder Management

Law and practice in the management of social housing
Desmond Kilcoyne, Barrister

"As a one-stop guide to leasehold management law, Desmond Kilcoyne's excellent book is clearly written, well set out, and each chapter concludes with useful pointers." *London Housing News*

"The purpose of this book is to help to equip the social landlord to perform one of the most difficult of all tasks: to keep a balance between the interests of tenants and of leaseholders; to be sure to provide leaseholders with no less than their legal rights, even when it is impracticable voluntarily to provide more to everyone – including the tenants; to understand and sympathetically to respond to disappointed expectations which may be common to others but which may be enhanced by an investment in proprietorship; and, to recognise that the forms of contemporary social housing irreversibly include owner-occupation, which means in turn that the very same people who immediately beforehand needed support as tenants may now need it even more."
Andrew Arden QC

Contents include:

Leaseholders, Leaseholds and Leases • The Legal Framework
• Service and Annual Charges • Service and Annual Charges • Major Works
• Service Charges and Improvement Contributions • Recovery of Service Charges • Covenants and Regulation of Management • Remedies of Landlord and Leaseholder • Change of Leaseholder or Landlord • Security of Tenure
• Enfranchisement and Extension of Long Leases

1997   ISBN 1-898001-10-3

Lemos & Crane books are obtainable from good bookshops or directly from
Plymbridge Distributors Ltd
Estover Road, Plymouth PL6 7PZ
• Tel: 01752 202301
• Fax: 01752 202333

Information about Arden's Housing Library and other Lemos & Crane books is available from
Lemos & Crane
20 Pond Square, London N6 6BA
• Tel: 0181-348 8263
• Fax: 0181-347 5740